lunch 13

Published by Applied Research and Design Publishing, an imprint of ORO Editions.
Gordon Goff: Publisher

www.appliedresearchanddesign.com
info@appliedresearchanddesign.com

Editors: Colin Gilliland, Kirk Gordon, Madelyn Hoagland-Hanson, Sarah Pate
Team: Alison Amos, Sam Kokenge, Aisha Sawatsky, Vida Shen, Taryn Wiens, Mengzhe Ye
Advising Editors: Megan Friedman, Sam Sidersky, Pia von Barby
Faculty Advisors: Bradley Cantrell, Sneha Patel
Project Manager: Jake Anderson

10 9 8 7 6 5 4 3 2 1 First Edition

ISBN: 978-1-941806-32-6

Color Separations and Printing: ORO Group Ltd.
Printed in China.

AR+D Publishing makes a continuous effort to minimize the overall carbon footprint of its publications. As part of this goal, AR+D, in association with Global ReLeaf, arranges to plant trees to replace those used in the manufacturing of the paper produced for its books. Global ReLeaf is an international campaign run by American Forests, one of the world's oldest nonprofit conservation organizations. Global ReLeaf is American Forests' education and action program that helps individuals, organizations, agencies, and corporations improve the local and global environment by planting and caring for trees.

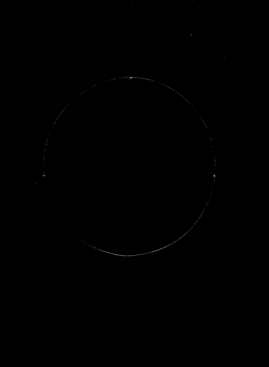

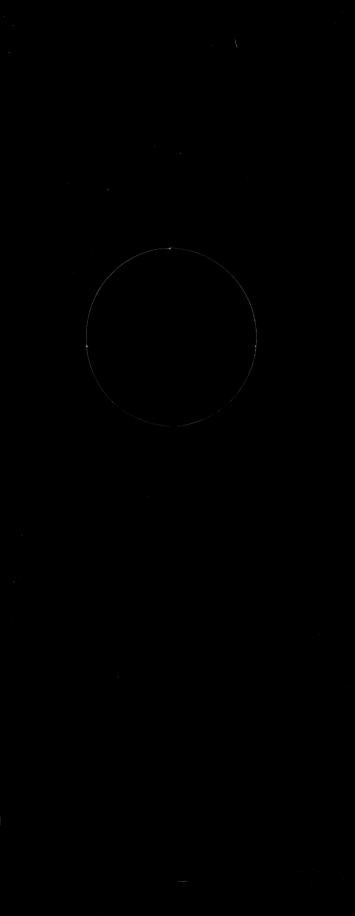

1
Adapted from "The Beginning of the Cree World," as told by the Saskatchewan Indigenous Cultural Center, http://www.sicc.sk.ca/archive/heritage/ethnography/cree/origin/oral.html.

To BEGIN, A TRICKSTER TALE[1]:

The Algonquin Cree of North America tell the story of Wisakedjak—commonly anglicized as "Whiskey Jack"—who angered the Creator by allowing men and animals to fight, spilling blood on the clean surface of the newly created Earth. The Creator warned Wisakedjak that if the bloodshed continued, he would be punished, but Wisakedjak didn't listen: he was having too much fun. The fighting went on, and the bloodshed continued, and gore and entrails were splattered all over the place.

The Creator gave Wisakedjak one more warning, but to no avail, and finally He had had it. He sent all the waters of the world to wash the Earth clean, an oceanic flood that drowned everyone and everything except for an Otter, a Beaver, a Muskrat, and Wisakedjak himself—all four of them bedraggled and clinging to a stray scrap of wood in the middle of an all-consuming sea.

Cool-headed and ever the silver-tongued charmer, Wisakedjak convinced all the animals in turn—first the Otter, then the Beaver, then the tiny Muskrat—to dive to the bottom of the sea and bring him a piece of the old Earth, the drowned Earth that had once been dry. From this he made a small island, and from there, remade the world.

In short, the trickster is a boundary crosser.

Every group has its edge, its sense of in and out, and trickster is always there, at the gates of the city and the gates of life, making sure there is commerce… We constantly distinguish—right and wrong, sacred and profane, clean and dirty, male and female, young and old, living and dead—and in every case trickster will cross the line and confuse the distinction.

Trickster is the creative idiot, therefore, the wise fool, the gray-haired baby, the cross-dresser, the speaker of sacred profanities. Where someone's sense of honorable behavior has left him unable to act, trickster will appear to suggest an amoral action, something right / wrong that will get life going again.

Trickster is the mythic embodiment of ambiguity and ambivalence, doubleness and duplicity, contradiction and paradox."

— Lewis Hyde, *Trickster Makes This World*

Prologue

1

For more on things, see Bill Brown, *Things* (Chicago: University of Chicago, 2004). For even more on things, see Bill Brown, *Other Things* (Chicago: University of Chicago, 2015).

2

According to the *New York Times*, the modern Wheel of Fortune mechanism is framed on a steel tube surrounded with Plexiglas and more than 200 lighting instruments. This assembly is held together by a stainless steel shaft with roller bearings. Altogether, the wheel weighs approximately 2,400 pounds. See Daniel E. Slotnik, "Ed Flesh, Designed the Wheel of Fortune, Dies at 79," *New York Times*, July 21, 2011.

3

See Serious Thing #91, page 120.

4

For more on weasels, see Natalie Angier, "Weasels Are Built for the Hunt," *New York Times*, June 13, 2016: "If they're well fed, Dr. Powell said, 'they'll bounce and ricochet around, pounce, stalk, wiggle and change shape and just about turn themselves inside out. They put kittens to shame.'"

5

See Sarah Netter, "Meep! Nonsense Word Goes Viral, Gets Students in Trouble," *ABC News*, Nov. 11, 2009: "[M]eeping doesn't seem to be funny to Danvers High School Principal Thomas Murray, who threatened to suspend students caught meeping."

6

Raoul Vanigem, *The Revolution of Everyday Life*, trans. Donald Nicholson-Smith (Seattle: Left Bank, 1967).

If the newspaper headlines are to be believed, Things[1]—generally speaking—Are Not Going Well. A Herculean hydra of global crises assaults us on all sides, invading every sphere of life from our courtrooms to our bedrooms. Nothing is sacred, nothing is safe, and nothing is making us feel any better. The moral high ground is getting harder to locate, what with those pesky melting ice caps and all. The Wheel of Fortune[2] has spun off its proverbial axis and is rolling right into the rising sea; in a few years we'll find it washed up on the Great Pacific Garbage Patch,[3] alongside ever-mounting piles of yesterday's news. In the corridors of power, a panicked whisper arises:

How are we going to get out of this one?

Glad you asked. In the midst of this festival of unrelenting awfulness, we proudly present the thirteenth issue of *lunch*, in which we summon the sleeping spirit of the Trickster. From Brer Rabbit to Raven, from Coyote to Anansi, from Hermes to Prometheus to Puck to Roadrunner, one thing all tricksters have in common is their capacity to weasel[4] out of the stickiest situations—and always with their sense of humor intact. Where solutionism falters, Trickster can be found, dancing delightedly between black and white. This is no time for moralizing, milquetoasting, and melodrama: this is the time to *meep-meep!*[5]

The essays, photos, drawings, and interviews within this volume approach the practice of mischief from multiple angles: from the political to the philosophical to the purely representational, they privilege the pleasurable, the provocative, and the seemingly pointless over the staid and corporate dreariness of partisan problem-solving. If, as Raoul Vaneigem[6] would have it, "to work on the side of delight and authentic festivity can hardly be distinguished from preparing for a general insurrection," we hope you delight in this issue of *lunch*.

On Friday the 13th of October 2017, the lunch *editorial board put out the following call for submissions:*

The STATE of THINGS is VERY SERIOUS.

The water is rising, the ice is melting, the forests are on fire, and the land is sinking. The storm is coming! The oceans are ACID! The fish are DYING! Trash is circling and circling in the widening gyre. Every day is a new catastrophe, we're rushing toward a precipice, we're out of time, we're out of luck, we screwed the pooch, dropped the ball, botched the delivery, broke the system, went hurtling down the road of good intentions—*we're sorry, officer—*

In design, we've been trained to respond with Solutions. So we've scaled up, we've made maps, we've run the numbers, we've analyzed the data, and aha! we found the answer: a 40-story apartment building made out of responsive mushroom bricks that cleans the air, collects stormwater, and hooks into a regional transit system to create a network of disruptive makerspaces that in turn will get to work on solving poverty.

"I've got you this time, Brer Rabbit," said Brer Fox, jumping up and shaking off the dust. "You've sassed me for the very last time. Now I wonder what I should do with you?"

Throughout history mischief makers have plagued the over-powerful, puncturing the smug assumptions of Fat Cats, Big Cheeses, and High Muck-a-Mucks. From Coyote to Anansi to Shakespeare's fools, the trickster holds the trump card when the chips are down, the stakes are high, and the owner of the casino is the President of the United States. We posit the wicked pleasures of the trickster tale as an enticing alternative to dreary disaster-capitalist narratives, technocratic solutionism, and universalist fictions of Authority, Progress, Unity, and Truth.

The editors of **lunch 13: Mischief** *cordially invite articles, letters, manifestos, anti-manifestos, quasi-manifestos, graphics, poems, comics, napkin sketches, recipes, games, and dirty jokes that approach design more impishly than urgently, that uproot assumptions that solutions are the solution, that wiggle under the garden fence and leave the farmer with a fistful of fur—but no bunny.*

"I was born and bred in the briar patch, Brer Fox," Brer Rabbit called. "Born and bred in the briar patch." And he skipped away as merry as a cricket while Brer Fox ground his teeth in rage and went home.

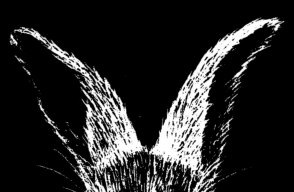

On Thu, Nov 2, 2017 at 11:40 AM, Marc Miller wrote:

Question—

Is there a particular reason you are using stories from Uncle Remus as part of the prompt? It seems to me that this is a questionable reference at best given the events in Charlottesville this past summer.

Respectfully,
Marc Miller

On Thu, Nov 2, 2017 at 4:03 PM, lunch-journal wrote:

Hi Marc,

Thank you for writing to us.

Our inclusion of the Brer Rabbit quotes was intentional; we realize they are provocative at best and offensive at worst in the wake of the white supremacist rallies here in Charlottesville this past summer. As students at the University of Virginia, we are confronted every day with the legacy of slavery and its particular role in shaping not only this school and its "founding father" but the American South (and America) more generally.

We wanted, through our inclusion of these quotes, to situate our journal in a particular place, with a particular history that often goes unacknowledged, at least in academic design forums—or when it is acknowledged, it is acknowledged as some kind of "niche" issue—as if "race" can be separated from history more generally. Our theme—"mischief"—is in part a response to what happened here in Charlottesville; we feel that mischief sometimes serves as political recourse for those who are marginalized in more traditional settings or institutions.

Our understanding (please correct us if this is wrong) of the Brer Rabbit stories is that they pre-date Joel Chandler Harris's appropriation of them in the form of the Uncle Remus stories, and that they have their roots in African folktales. They are of course not just stories but (in a sense) coded messages, and served as a way for slaves to communicate hard-won lessons in a form that evaded the understanding of their masters. In her essay "Uncle Remus, No Friend of Mine," Alice Walker describes the lesson she derived from her mother's telling of the Tar Baby story as follows:

> *Now we begin to suspect that Brer Fox's hatred of Brer Rabbit is greater than his hunger. It is more important to him that Brer Rabbit suffer than that he himself be satisfied. Of course, he runs and finds the nearest briar patch and flings Brer Rabbit into it. Once unstuck from the tar baby and on the ground, Brer Rabbit laughs at Brer Fox and says, "I was born and raised in the briar patch, born and raised in the briar patch." And of course he gets away.*

1

Alice Walker, "Uncle Remus, No Friend of Mine," *The Georgia Review* 66, no. 3 (2012): 635-637.

No matter how many times I heard this story as a child, I always expected Brer Fox to be able to use his considerable intelligence to help himself, rather than expend all his energy trying to harm Brer Rabbit. But my parents' point, and that of the story, was: This is the nature of Brer Fox, and a smart rabbit will never forget it.[1]

In the same essay, Walker describes the trauma of her experience of the appropriation of the Brer Rabbit stories by white people—in particular by Walt Disney's *Song of the South*: "As far as I'm concerned, [Joel Chandler Harris] stole a good part of my heritage. How did he steal it? By making me feel ashamed of it. In creating Uncle Remus, he placed an effective barrier between me and the stories that meant so much to me, the stories that could have meant so much to all of our children, the stories that they would have heard from us and not from Walt Disney."[2]

2

Ibid.

We know that to reference the written form of these stories (which were inherently oral, and therefore inherently intimate) is to immediately misappropriate and perhaps misuse them. But the stories themselves have agency that pre-dates and in some sense transcends the racist caricature of Uncle Remus invented by Joel Chandler Harris to diminish and reduce them to ridicule. We want to re-surface, not ridicule, Brer Rabbit in all of his volatile power; we want to evoke not only the original power of the stories, but also the "slow violence" of their appropriation.

In using the Brer Rabbit quotations, we realized we were treading a dangerous line; we decided among ourselves that the conversation that might arise from using the quotes was worth the risk. We are interested in your reaction to both our use of the quotation and possibly to the theme more generally. As it stands, you are one of the only people who has questioned or commented on our use of the quotes, which is surprising to us considering our initial hesitation.

Thanks again for your email. Hope to hear from you.

Maddie & the *lunch* 13 Editorial Board

Regarding the Briar Patch: An Open Letter

Marc Miller

To the 2018 Editorial Board,

This fall I considered the call for *Mischief* with confusion. Your use of Brer Rabbit as a prompt was indeed uncomfortable, given the historical significance of the stories. In this spirit, I'd like to return to that original brief email exchange and offer up some points regarding the larger systemic and spatial conditions—the Briar Patch—within which this all resonates.

First, I would like to suggest that your reading of Brer Rabbit is that of the appropriated character. The excerpts that you have chosen to use are the refined portrayal of a hero that is in control, even in a situation that might lead to significant harm. Placed in context, this is yet another story of exceptionalism, the ability of the individual to overcome the adversities placed in front of him. This is not the character of oral history; this is a hero that Joel Chandler Harris crafted by appropriating those stories for his benefit.

I'd argue that this is another barrier that Harris places between African-Americans and the Briar Patch. The narrative of exceptionalism derived from the appropriated Brer Rabbit stories has been used as a device to reveal collective racial shortcomings, ignoring the systemic prejudices at the heart of continuing inequality. But heroic exceptionalism was not the purpose of Brer Rabbit stories; these were cautionary tales. This wasn't just storytelling to pass the time but an effort by enslaved people to teach their children how to behave with slave owners to maximize their personal safety. Brer Rabbit was an educational meme, not an individual hero; by placing emphasis on an idealized individual, the collective becomes increasingly removed from this narrative. In short, I'd argue that there wasn't one but many rabbits in the Briar Patch, a distinction that Chandler's appropriation erases.

This brings me to my second point regarding the problematic suggestion that Brer Rabbit was capable of using force as a form of agency. This suggestion reinforces the reading of him as a hero, but it also implies that earlier audiences of slaves were capable of mustering up some form of force that would not immediately lead to personal harm. Referencing the story used in the prompt, Brer Rabbit exerts force only against the tar baby, and even then, is defeated. His only action is to retreat into the anonymity of the Briar Patch, a place he is familiar with. He knows the ins and outs of that space better than any fox, both out of familiarity and out of necessity.

To place this in a larger context, consider the spatial and social implications of being a descendant of slaves. Recall that the hanging of Denmark Vesey[1] after he was convicted of conspiracy in a secret trial was followed by the burning of Emanuel African Methodist Episcopal (AME) Church to dispel any other hopes of a coup. Think how repeatedly that single church has been subsequently visited with violence "as a reminder," most recently in the form of a mass killing during a prayer meeting.[2]

In a contemporary context, think of the accusations being leveled against groups like Black Lives Matter because the organizers spoke out regarding the disproportionate number of deaths among people who look like descendants of slaves. Think of Jim Crow laws, Plessy versus Ferguson, and Brown versus Board of Education, and how these rules of law had violent impacts on the formerly enslaved and their descendants—descendants of Brer Rabbit—in the form of lynchings, church burnings, and landscape/architectures with minimal access to basic infrastructural needs.

Considering this, there has not been a moment when they have been allowed volatile power. Volatile actions are a privilege, as is the case with what appears to be confrontational behavior. To suggest that Brer Rabbit would have been afforded this privilege again points to the misinterpretation of the character as a hero and not a "device."

In all this thinking about Brer Rabbit and the Briar Patch, drawings of shotgun shack communities keep popping into my head. I'm not focused on the building form—long narrow boxes with entrances on the ends to assist in corralling the occupants—so much as their urban assemblies. Specifically, I'm imagining the densely packed buildings with irregular depths and narrow passages on the side, irregular because raiding parties would have a harder time chasing people through the spaces and anticipating where they would exit. The block pattern of these communities (as illustrated in Steven Holl's *Pamphlet Architecture 7: Bridge of Houses*) demonstrates the irregular arrangement of building

1
Michael P. Johnson, "Denmark Vesey and His Co-Conspirators." *The William and Mary Quarterly* 58, no. 4 (2001): 915-76.

2
David Von Drehle, Jay Newton, and Maya Rhodan, "Charleston Shooting Cover Story," *Time,* http://time.com/time-magazine-charleston-shooting-cover-story/.

footprints around a central open space that afforded access to all the properties—provided that you know where you were going. The architecture might have been one of control, but the arrangement was determined to deter access into the interior, giving residents passive control of their place.

3
Ta-Nehisi Coates, "The Case for Reparations," *The Atlantic*, August 17, 2017, https://www.theatlantic.com/magazine/archive/2014/06/the-case-for-reparations/361631/.

I also think about Ta-Nehisi Coates's article, "The Case for Reparations,"[3] in which he documents the calculated denial of property—and therefore wealth—to African Americans. I think about the stories he tells of people who moved from southern cities to northern cities when their property was seized from them, only to have the same done to them again in the form of predatory purchasing conditions. I think about how governmental programs such as the GI Bill and Farm Loans were withheld from descendants of slaves, through calculated "missteps" and omissions. I think about the establishment of the National Black Farmers Association in 1995 and the subsequent campaign of church burning comparable if not rivaling the arsons witnessed during the Civil Rights Era.

These are all evidence of the "slow violence" you refer to. Is this because we choose to see the actors in these events through the lens of Harris's Brer Rabbit, consoled in the confidence that someone will step forward and become that clever trickster? All this is a long-winded way of asking what kind of mischief you are looking for—and from whom? After all, mischief is not a right so much as it is an affordance—like identity, security, and authorship. Harris's Brer Rabbit was afforded these qualities through appropriation and exceptionalism. This is not the same rabbit that lives in worry, not so much trying to be clever as just trying to stay alive in the Briar Patch. This rabbit doesn't have the security of place—let alone the privilege—to be mischievous.

This makes me curious as to what you will accept as mischief.

Marc Miller
December 20, 2017

"Tactical Frivolity": A Conversation with Artúr van Balen

The Editors

Kirk (L): Your organization, Tools for Action, approaches activism by engaging art, spectacle, and collective performance. How did you arrive at this particular mode of engagement and where did you find your inspiration?

Artúr (A): Well, I suppose it began when I was in art school. There weren't many professors of sculpture at the time, and the few we had were often absent. But there were these "free classes"—self-organized classes where students would teach one another and work on a group-initiated project. We formed a new group, and were given a small budget, and we began to think of how we might make these inflatable "air castles" as a way of representing a kind of utopian space. But something that you can't quite reach, that is not yet concrete, but still sort of floating above you. And I found the collective building process with that to be really joyful. That was in 2007. In 2009, I began to get involved in climate activism and on-site direct action. Through this I learned how to carry out media spectacles, and to think about how you can protest through performative acts, and gain attention through surprising actions and narratives. In 2010 we worked to support the protest for the International Climate Conference in Cancun. We weren't able to fly there, however, so we built a 12-meter inflatable hammer, folded it up in a suitcase, and sent it over to a friend who put it in the hands of a Mexican climate activist group. They inflated it on the day of action and ran with it through the barrier between the protestors and the conference area. It was destroyed by the police in front of a Reuters media journalist and within three hours it had

become an icon of climate change protests internationally. So through that we really began to understand how inflatables could create media spectacles, but also how they could serve as an ironic commentary on the media spectacle itself, given that events are often inflated to gigantic proportions then quickly "deflate" and disappear.

At that time we were called Electric Collective, and this was basically our first inflatable tool. It was inspired by a dictum of a Russian Constructivist poet, Vladimir Mayakovsky, from the 1920s, who said, "Art is not a mirror to society but a hammer with which to shape it." From this we formed the position that if you want to do political art, it is not enough to represent reality. You have to actually intervene. It became the inspiration for the next generation of inflatable tools, which we made in partnership with other artists and activist groups. And in 2012, I founded Tools for Action, which serves generally as a collaborative platform under which I engage with other art and activist groups, theaters, and even schools.

L: It's quite interesting to hear that the inflatable's origin is grounded in this attempt to conceptualize a utopian space. The making of these inflatables becomes both a literal and metaphorical act of building, of envisioning the future. This is what we as architects are always attempting to do. It's fascinating to observe this evolution of form from the castle, as a kind of vernacular architecture, to the hammer, as a tool for building, to the current form—these cubes or bricks—which represent a material unit for construction. You've managed to find power and agency in each of these separate aspects.

**Are there other forms or prototypes you're currently working with,
or have you focused recently on the cube shape alone?**

A: Ha, yes, it would seem I'm a bit stuck in inflatable cubism. This
started in 2012, when we were invited to a Spanish art activists festival
in Barcelona called *Cómo acabar con el Mal* ("How To End Evil"). There
was a general strike happening at the time—the whole city was on strike
against austerity measures. We made this inflatable cube, and when the
riot police came, we threw the cube against the police line. They bounced
it back at the crowd, and suddenly there was this involuntary moment of
play. We had put them in a kind of decision dilemma, in which they had
only a limited number of choices. They could throw the inflatable back,
creating a condition of playful interaction; they could try to destroy it,
making them look rather foolish and aggressive for attacking a balloon,
or they could "arrest" the balloon, which they actually tried to do. They
attempted to take the whole balloon and try to squeeze it into the police
van. So the cube created this empowerment of the protestor, a flipping
of the coin, in which the protestor gained authority over the interaction.
We transformed the archetype of the aggressive, stone-throwing protestor
into a more empowered, positive actor. Spanish social movements picked
up on this, and it became a huge success. We repeated it again later in
Berlin.

The cube is one of the most basic shapes to make. It's very easy
to reproduce, helping us to expand the scope of action through
decentralized production. People anywhere can follow a few online
tutorials and easily create their own. But we're still updating the cubes,

fig. 4
Protesters launch inflatables during a protest of the 2015 United Nations International Climate Change Conference in Paris, France. (Photo: Artúr van Balen)

kind of like a software that upgrades. In 2015, we were asked to create soft blockades for the protest of the International Climate Conference in Paris. Paris is actually the inventor of the barricade, invented on May 12, 1588: The Day of the Barricades. Barricade actually comes from the French word *barrique*, which means barrel. The public, in frustration with the king's policies, had gotten into the revolutionary spirit after a few drinks, and rolled the *barriques* onto the street, reinforcing them with metal chains and filling them with stones. Eventually they drove the king out. So for Paris, we created extra handles on the cubes, and Velcro for reinforcement.

But essentially, the cube serves as a metaphor for the people in the community. People make the cubes and then they can all gather together to create this modular wall structure, which you can extend and extend—indefinitely. So that's really another reason for the cubes—the idea that a community of like-minded people can gather to create something bigger. The inflatable is born from and creates a social body. You build it together and carry it together, and the conjunction of these conditions creates a social cohesion. And we noticed something really interesting in Paris when we tried this. The protest took place just after a terrorist attack, so protests were really not allowed at that moment. But it still happened as an act of disobedience. There were 8,000 people on the streets, with 35 cubes and 60 activists from different groups all connected by a phone tree. We discussed where the cubes go and what the options for collective performance were. We first created a wall structure, but then later disassembled it and threw the cubes up in the air. And the cubes simply rolled down the street, bouncing overtop of people and the crowd. And when a balloon comes toward you, you automatically just bounce it further. So we observed this emergent pattern, this choreographic reverberation that we found quite interesting.

The inflatable is born from and creates a social body. You build it together and carry it together, and the conjunction of these conditions creates a social cohesion.

Yet another update to the inflatable cube came on invitation of the Theater of Dortmund, after the local neo-Nazi scene called for an international neo-Nazi demonstration in the city. You could call it the German version of the "Unite the Right" rally. Dortmund is infamous for their militant neo-Nazi scene. In the 1980s, this neo-Nazi scene started to take root there, and since then the city has become an organizing center in West Germany. Since 2000, six people have been killed. The city's inhabitants live in this fear, a fear that grows under the skin. In 2016, there was an enormous desire to act against this neo-Nazi demonstration. So we created a mirror barricade. We put reflective material on the cube to reflect the violence and hatred of the neo-Nazi community back onto them, but also to serve as a reminder for everyone to reflect on our own position. At the same, the barricades served to blockade the march, for those people who were willing to commit acts of civil disobedience. So this encompassed the desires of many people who were not interested in the traditional forms of protests, but found inspiration in this new form of engagement. Hundreds of people helped to make the cubes, from activists to priests, and we practiced different choreographies together. This was also the first time we actually conducted workshops in schools on how to build barricades, which was very interesting. We were basically giving students a taste for collective organizing and taking action, and what it might mean to put your own body in the line for a political motivation. Which I think is very important in our digital, disembodied, anonymous times.

L: Since you've begun to identify material updates to the cube, can you explain more about the types of materials that you use?

A: Yes, so as a base material for the hammer, we used aluminum insulation foil, which is commonly used for the insulation of houses. This was the tip of an inflatable architect friend, Marco Carnevacci, from the group Plastique Fantastique. The good thing about it is that is has a mesh wire in it, so it has a certain stability. And the silver reflectivity makes it attractive. And also, because it is used in the building industry, it is cheap and widely available. So, as a way to support the idea of decentralized production, it was very suitable. This is also the reason we use double stick carpet tape as a way to reinforce the seams of the cubes, since it is also very low-tech and widely accessible. We have also begun to use some plastic at times—PVC, unfortunately.

L: Could you talk more about the spatial logics of the inflatables— the way they actually change our conceptualization of space through movement?

A: Well, generally, the idea of inflatable architecture stems from the 1970s from this idea of pop-up architecture, or the creation of temporary autonomous zones. After the Second World War, synthetic plastics came on the market, and it became possible to use and experiment with this inflatable technology. In the U.S., a collective called Ant Farm was formed. They were this kind of San Francisco flower-power architect group, and later became a media activist group as well. They created the InflatoCookbook, a manual for how to make inflatable spaces, in 1970. A number of similar groups began to pop up, too, all around 1968. In Vienna there was Haus-Rucker-Co and Coop Himmelblau. Paris had the UTOPIE group. There was the UFO group in Florence, Italy, and Archigram in the UK. So we entertain a lot of positions from the '70s and use them to inform our own. With Tools for Action, we are more interested in the idea of gatherings of people, such as at protests. But we are also interested in the idea of performance. This inspiration came in 2009, when I was part of a protest in Copenhagen at the climate conference. There was a demonstration which stopped in front of the city hall, and all of a sudden there was this big advertisement balloon that got caught by the wind, and hundreds of people started to run with it! People started to run through the city like a social amoeba, choreographed by the wind. For me this was an example of how inflatables attract crowds and can create crowd unity in a very spontaneous way. Something that trade unionists do elaborate studies on—inflatables can do just like that!

Of course, this is also wrapped up in a deeper, more psychological phenomenon. As children, we are always fascinated with big balloons. It is something quite large in relation to our own body, but at the same time light and playful. And I think people, and policemen, are somehow brought back to their inner-child state when they are confronted with these massive, lightweight objects. They create these surreal moments which break us out from our daily habits and routines. They inspire us to think about how reality might be different, and to imagine what else is possible. It's a kind of material resistance. And at the same time, the inflatable also has an agency all its own, existing and moving with this kind of autonomous magnetism. It's something you can't really describe well in words, I find. It's really something you must experience.

As children, we are always fascinated with big balloons. It is something quite large in relation to our own body, but at the same time light and playful.

L: Yes, I love this idea of material resistance, and how materials produce their own kinds of autonomous effects. There's this interesting thing I've noticed in watching your protest footage where, as the inflatables begin to deflate, they start to give a little bit when hit, making them even harder for police to swat away. They transform from these bright, active, boisterous beings to these

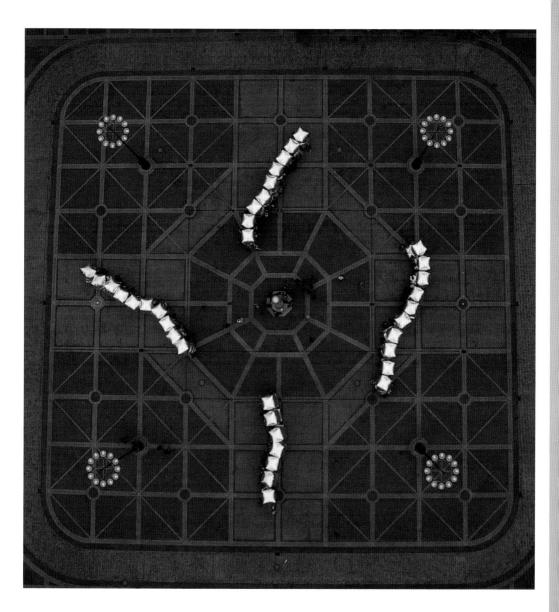

fig. 5

Demonstrators of all ages perform a
"barricade ballet" at Wilhelmsplatz
square in Dortmund, self-proclaimed
by local neo-Nazis as their "national
liberated zone."
(Photo: Tools for Action)

hilariously lethargic, cumbersome creatures. That said, despite them acting as physical barriers, they are in reality a rather fragile aggregation of materials. So it does seem to me that the inflatables command a strength and presence that goes beyond their material reality, and that much of it is psychological.

But going back to this idea of gathering and choreography—I've noticed in some of your writing that you've spoken about theories of crowd emergence. Can you elaborate on that?

A: Paris was a very unique moment for us, where the cubes were organically taken up and propelled through the crowd. The movement was in part initiated by our group members, but it was also perpetuated in a large way by this spontaneous emergent behavior that grew from the 8,000-person crowd. This inspired us to think, "Wow, could they really induce some kind of emergent crowd movement or patterns?"

fig. 6 (facing)
A school workshop in Dortmund.
(Photo: Artúr van Balen)

fig. 7
A school workshop in Dortmund.
(Photo: Bandermann)

But to simulate that again is very difficult, regardless of the fact that you rarely have a crowd of that size together. In Dortmund, we did the barricades action training with around 250 people and more than 100 cubes, and it was far more directed. "Now we do a wall. Now let's do Asterix and Obelix (old style military formations)." So it was much less emergent. We're still experimenting in this emergent direction. Maybe emerging isn't even the right word—perhaps it is better to call them non-hierarchical or non-directed movement patterns. But there's always a resonance between directed and non-directed events.

What we're experimenting with now, especially in regards to climate activism, is to motivate action in the younger generation through school workshops and such. One idea is to see if 5th or 6th grade kids can self-organize and direct their own choreographies. We've also been teaching them to control drones and to create their own imagery. We want to give them the tools to create political spectacle and to grab the attention of social media. Through this they learn the creative techniques for interventions in public space and in politics. Our hope is that one day, when they're angry and want to protest something, that they'll remember and have the knowledge of how to do it in a more creative, joyful, and empowering way.

L: Yes, I think the ability to collectively influence and direct the media narrative has become a huge part of protesting today. It has become more and more important for us to reassert our own power over the media, and despite its flaws, social media remains an essential platform for young people to work together and amplify their collective voice.

fig. 8
Counter-protest training with the
community in Dortmund.
(Photo: Regenfrei Productions)

Can you talk a little bit more about the training sessions that you've conducted, and the different types of groups you've gathered to build the inflatables? It seems like these gatherings are used not just to build the barricades, but to facilitate broader discussions about the issues at hand.

A: Yes. The basic idea is that building the inflatables creates a social sculpture. It is interesting for artists who simply want to learn how to fabricate the inflatables, but it also attracts activists who want to achieve something politically and gain attention. In Dortmund we saw firsthand how it could be really intergenerational, and open for everyone to engage in. Plus, it provides a different means of communication than just, say, holding a political meeting. It's a bit more relaxed. Particularly with the school workshops, it has been important to have broader discussions about political issues and activism. In Dortmund, we engaged students in discussions about the neo-Nazi ideology and community in their city, and tried to flesh out what their ideas where regarding what is German, in order to deconstruct all these racist attitudes and leave space for open discussions.

What was interesting on that particular Day of Action is that we made it possible for you to borrow a barricade kit of six cubes, and you could decide for yourself which demonstration you would go to. For instance, there was the direct counter-demonstration, which had proclaimed that they would be performing civil disobedience, and were going to directly stop the neo-Nazi march. But there was also the more moderate trade union demonstration, who had chosen to build up a wall of mirrored barricades as more of a symbolic sign of protest. You could also perform your own self-organized action. But all of this worked as a form of political education, encouraging people to position themselves within a political space, within a particular demonstration, and to reflect on where

fig. 9
Counter-protesters create a
barricade to block a neo-Nazi march
in Dortmund, Germany.
(Photo: Flint Stelter)

they were positioning themselves in regards to this problem. It allowed for lots of discussion afterwards in terms of political effectiveness. And the instructors we work with come from backgrounds in activism. They have a lot of experience, especially with civil disobedience and doing things that are not average. So we try to inspire people to think differently and to act differently. There is this development of various critical tools, centered around the creation of a physical tool. And in this way it allows us to have much deeper conversations, rather than just talking about the issue in the abstract.

L: What I admire about the process is that every part of it is an act of collective building, from the production of material units, to their transportation and assemblage, and finally to their demolition, as seen when the cubes were spread through the crowd in Paris. As you know, Charlottesville has been struggling with our own legacies of bigotry and white supremacy, which culminated in a horrific and tragic confrontation last August. I'm reflecting on the boiling tension and sheer frustration of that event and am wondering what role inflatables might have been able to play there. What do

fig. 10

Inflatables mediate between counter-protesters & police in Dortmund.
(Photo: Flint Stelter)

you think is the importance of introducing play or lightness into situations like these?

A: Well, first of all, I must assert that the inflatable barricades work more as a visual barricade, and to a certain extent a temporary physical barrier. But they cannot save a person when a car is driving through a crowd. We must remember that, as a protestor, you actually might not see that well with the cubes if you become implicated in a situation as dangerous and horrible as that. So this is a problem in certain situations. But it can also be a strength.

When you throw them in the air, it turns the street into a playground. I think of the Paris '68 riots and the phrase "sous les paves, le plage"— "under the pavement, the beach." The inflatables can help break the tension and change the dynamic, for suddenly there is this other body in between, mediating things. By breaking the scripted or expected routine of confrontational protests, you can work to puncture a situation and de-escalate it. This is one of the hopes. This is also why it can be good to bring just one even, as it creates an immediate response of participation and a sort of mascot for crowd solidarity. Additionally, they're very visually impressive, and can take away the spotlight from the aesthetic of neo-fascist rallies, with their candles and torches and such. So I see them as just one tactic that can and should be used among other tactics, in different situations. It's more about taking all these big objects and symbolizing the collective body of resistance, or creating a visual symbol of the scale of resistance. In this way they help in certain situations. But they are not a solution to anything, necessarily.

L: Yes, I really appreciate the reminder that this is one tactic among many. As we continue to talk about the idea of spectacle and its political utility, I think it is important to acknowledge the recent rise of political technologists and the daily fabrications of politicians like Putin and Trump. Media spectacle is at the top of their toolkit when it comes to public deception and distraction. So I feel like it's intelligent and pragmatic for you to embrace spectacle yourself. Activism requires an awareness of the tactics by which injustices proliferate, and I think it's important for us to identify and co-opt these tactics ourselves as a form of resistance.

A: Yes, certainly. I was inspired by a theorist/activist from New York, Stephen Duncombe, who wrote the book *Dream: Reimagining Progressive Politics in the Age of Fantasy*. There he argues that creating spectacle has been used by authoritarian states and by advertisement, but that progressive movements must also create spectacles because we are in an attention economy. So, we cannot treat spectacle as purely bad, or just distraction, in the way Guy DeBord and the Situationists proclaimed in the seventies. Duncombe makes a claim for the "ethical spectacle," which is not only seductive but ethical through its transparency. The community who makes the spectacle is aware and open about how they are making it and, in this way, it is an empowering strategy. I see the cube-making in a similar way. Many people together make the cubes, which are really just an empty shell. But we fill it with our own meaning while we do it. We speak and listen to one another, and create this community that is manifested in our creation. Then, later, the larger viewing audience gives it an expanded meaning. The spectacle is simply a way of creating strong imagery, for creating collective symbols and memetic solidarity.

L: There is another term that I've seen you use that I really love, something you call "tactical frivolity." Can you explain what this means?

A: It's basically the idea of coercing authority into a decision dilemma, as we did with the police and that first cube. They are forced to engage with what is essentially a big balloon. No matter their response, their authority is temporarily undermined and they are made to look foolish. So in this way, the inflatables are a tool for creating temporary, liberating moments within a space and a public that are increasingly controlled. And as I mentioned before, the inflatables themselves are autonomous. We cannot fully control them, but they are affecting and influencing us, as well as responding to other factors such as wind. The simple recognition that we cannot fully control this thing becomes a liberating moment for everyone, and that's why they remain fascinating to me. 🐰

A Modest Request for Proposals

Sam Johnson

fig. 1 (facing)
Detail from "Dinner Theater"
Proposal, OMG Architects (Darcy
Engle)

Recently our company sent out the following request for proposals regarding our desire to build a new Swift Foods flagship location. Because we feel that this building will serve to move both our company and our community forward, and because the design proposals we received were so strong, we have decided to open up the competition to public voting. Please feel free to take this opportunity to read over our prompt, review the following proposals, and submit your vote! And if you feel like it, take the time to visit our website. We hope you'll feel as strongly about our products as we do!

Note:
The following responses to the
author's RFP were submitted by
students at the University of Virginia
and Parsons School of Design.

SECTION A CONTINUATION - SOLICITATION/CONTRACT FORM SF 2083 CONSTRUCTION DESIGN/BUILD

I. REQUEST FOR PROPOSALS

Swift Foods is requesting proposals from qualified firms or individuals to provide design proposals for a new headquarters and production facility with the potential for additional program, as outlined later in the prompt.

II. ABOUT OUR BRAND

It is a melancholy object, our society's ever-widening income gap. Low-income, menial jobs upon which so many families used to depend are increasingly being rendered obsolete through innovations in technology, design, and globalization. While a boon for society as a whole, these developments have taken a toll on many of the impoverished families that constitute Middle America; these families are increasingly without the means and the motivation to procure work, unable or unwilling to learn the necessary skills to compete in the marketplace. This is to say nothing of today's youth, who, although tech-savvy, are far too concerned with their social media presence to truly devote themselves to a career. Indeed, if the current generation of low-income adults is unable to overcome their current socioeconomic conditions, there is no hope for their children.

As unfortunate as these circumstances may be, we see a solution that would benefit those individuals able to make something of themselves in today's America and provide a use and a purpose for those poor children who have no marketable skills.

Swift Foods was explicitly founded to take advantage of this niche in the market and to disrupt the food industry by creating an organic, wholesome alternative to the traditional meat product, consisting entirely of these heretofore-useless children.

III. PROJECT ABSTRACT

In order to move forward with Swift Food's vision for a healthy, genuinely American food experience, the company seeks a new flagship headquarters and production facility. This will serve not only as the primary location for the preparation and sale of child meat, but also ideally as an urban nexus, a location where both employee and consumer can congregate and enjoy a hearty meal.

The facility should provide, at minimum, space for the following; office space for 50-100 employees, conference rooms, detainment area, private offices for 5-10 members of upper management, employee cafeteria, killing floor, processing line, and a daycare. More specific requirements and projected square footages are included in the appendix.

Swift Foods welcomes proposals that include other programs within the project. Firms should feel free to include residential units both for the high-end clientele who will constitute a large portion of the company's consumer base and for those families that will provide the sustenance. We find that today's savvy eater increasingly wants to know where and how their food was raised; the farm-to-table movement has become very popular.

Obviously, to avoid logistical mishaps, separate entrances should be provided.

IV. EXPERIENCE AND QUALIFICATIONS

- Each Architect submitting a proposal should include, but not be limited to, the following information:

- The name of the firm and location of all its offices; priority will be given to firms located in coastal cities, as it is a well-acknowledged fact that these cities have the greatest vantage point from which to see what is best for Middle America, the residents of which will undoubtedly provide much of the stock for the company.

- The age of the firm, and the total number of years providing architectural services. Priority will be given to firms with experience in designing prisons, slaughterhouses, or at the very least, high-end residential.

- Names and résumés of key members of the firm who will be expected to lead the project. Because our company is investing a lot of time and money into this project, specific members will be expected to attend biweekly site meetings. Lunch will be provided.

- Swift Foods has already retained the services of two consultants for the project; APUP Engineering and Bronson Sausage Stuffers. Prior experience working with either is considered a plus.

V. EVALUATION CRITERIA AND SELECTION

Swift Foods will evaluate each submitted proposal based on responsiveness to the project's needs. It also encourages and appreciates the ability of the firm to look beyond the minimum requirements of the prompt. Firms that address some of the following issues will be preferred:

- If the architect is able to locate a suitable building, Swift Foods would be interested in the potential for the adaptive reuse of an existing structure. Whether it be the skeleton of an unused warehouse or the skeleton of a child, Swift Foods tries to eliminate waste in all aspects of the business.

- Projects which propose environmentally sustainable features or achieve LEED certification will be greatly preferred. Swift Foods is of course very concerned with the future of the planet and would like its headquarters to reflect these priorities.

- The opportunity for the facility to serve as a transit hub should be considered. Said hub could tie into existing public transit options or serve as the base for a company fleet of vehicles. Companies such as Google and Facebook have already had great success with similar concepts in cities such as Berkeley, where the homeless are all but devoured already.

- Ample outdoor space would be looked upon favorably. Consumers prefer the taste of free-range foods, and research has shown that the calcium-rich bones of young children can be a boon to various types of vegetation.

Entry 01

"Beyond the Traditional Pasture Circumstance"

Firm: LIKN Architects

Project Architects: Aisha Sawatsky & Emily Fiedler

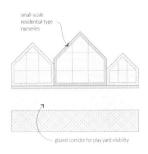

small-scale residential-type nurseries

glazed corridor for play yard visibility

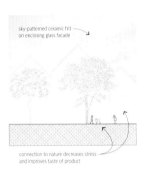

sky-patterned ceramic frit on enclosing glass facade

connection to nature decreases stress and improves taste of product

play structure facilitates positive feelings prior to harvesting in Yard 4

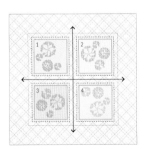

products separated by age with visibility to other yards to encourage aspiring to final Yard 4

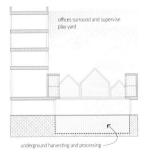

offices surround and supervise play yard

underground harvesting and processing

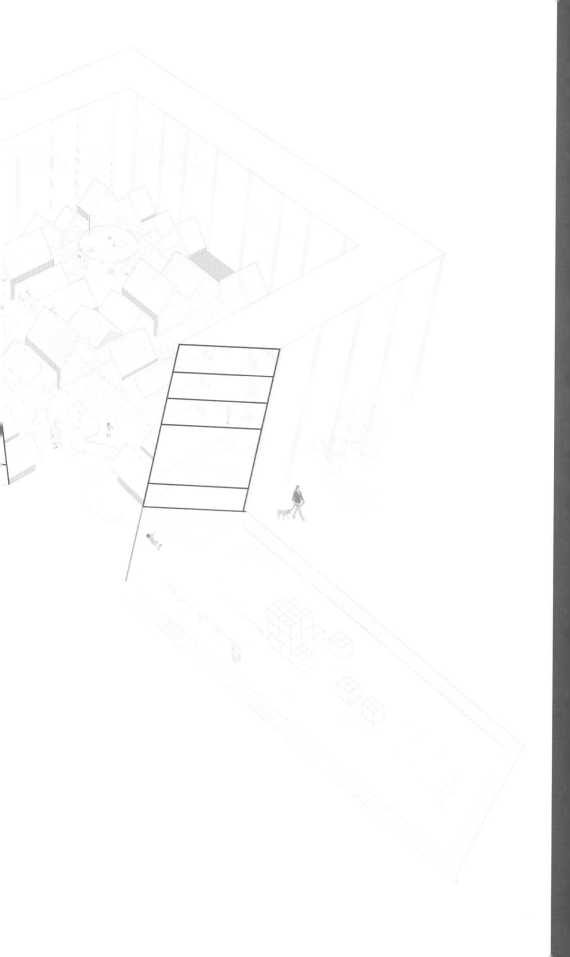

Entry 02

"Swift Foods Processing Tower"

Firm: CHoP Architects

Project Architect: Angela DeGeorge

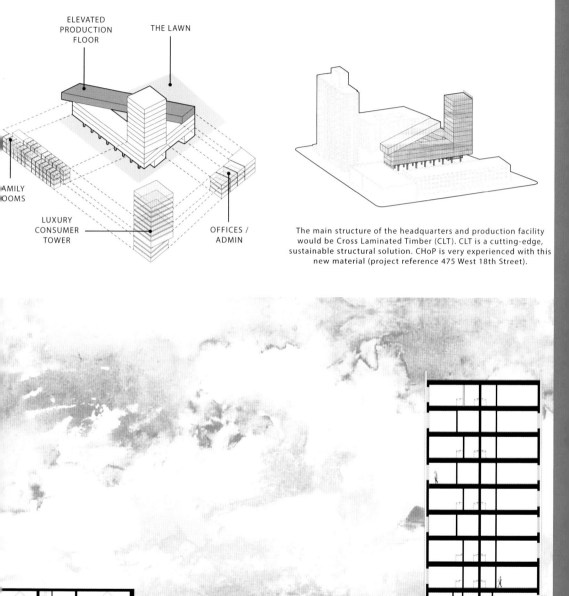

ELEVATED
PRODUCTION
FLOOR

THE LAWN

AMILY
OOMS

LUXURY
CONSUMER
TOWER

OFFICES /
ADMIN

The main structure of the headquarters and production facility would be Cross Laminated Timber (CLT). CLT is a cutting-edge, sustainable structural solution. CHoP is very experienced with this new material (project reference 475 West 18th Street).

DETAINMENT AREA DA

EVENT SPACE
KITCHEN
MARKET PR
DINING AREA

RE

SALES OFFICES

IAGEMENT OFFICES CONFERENCE ROOMS

BACK STAGE

NNER

IEATER

CT TESTING

PACKAGING

PRODUCTION LINES

BREAKROOM   LOADING DOCKS

EMPLOYEE CAFETERIA

Entry 04
"The Playpen"
Firm: DDRDMV
Project Architect: Sherry Ng

DDRDMV

In moving towards the difficult whole,
inclusiveness has become exhausted,
and we should rather move to relate
to the context beyond. In a sense
these bad spaces can be thought of
as just a compromise for the sake
of the whole. The decisions of such
valid compromises are one of the chief
tasks of the architect. I regret such
a decision to be made, but as it
must be done, in the very least
should it not be of the limitations
of orthodox Modern architecture, in the style of
populizers who paint fairy stories
over our chaotic reality.

R V '18

Afterword: Why Satire?

Since Jonathan Swift published *A Modest Proposal*—his satirical essay suggesting the commodification and consumption of poor Irish youths as a solution for economic woes— in 1729, surprisingly few scholars have formally analyzed the piece, despite its lasting impact on the satirical essay and Western humor as a whole. George Wittkowsky claims that this absence derives largely from a misinterpretation of its subject matter. "If one regards *A Modest Proposal* simply as a criticism of conditions," he writes, "about all one can say is that conditions were bad and that Swift's irony brilliantly underscored this fact."[1] Wittkowsky, however, does not regard *A Modest Proposal* so simply. He points to the fact that, in the few years directly preceding Swift's essay, numerous genuine economic proposals were published, many of which had titles starting with phrases such as "a humble proposition" or "a modest proposal." Swift's "proposal" in this light then becomes not merely a humorous exaggeration of existing conditions, but a scathing critique of the flawed and incomplete logic he saw around him.

Why has this facet of its satire been overlooked so consistently? Both at the time and in the succeeding decades, this era was not considered to have had an overarching economic theory. Yet Swift was able to identify and lambaste certain characteristics consistent across the various economic writings at the time: the promotion of child labor as an important sector of the economy, the notion that "the people are the riches of the land," and an importance placed on the number of people employed, regardless of the quality of the wages and working conditions. (You may notice here that the first of these notions seems completely outrageous, and the last, unfortunately, persists as an ideology.) Swift was able, through the use of satire, to not only draw attention to the flaws present in these economic dictums, but importantly, to define a previously unexamined ideology through humor.

In some ways, architectural philosophy suffers from a lack of definition similar to that of the economic philosophy in Swift's era. There is no doubt that certain aspects of architectural philosophy have been sufficiently explored; much has been written about the modalities of design in architecture, the ideological implications of certain formal or material decisions, and the ways these decisions influence individual and communal actions. Yet despite this, much remains to be said about the ethical implications of practicing architecture.

For many architects, once they enter into practice, program becomes a static, intractable object. Program can help to guide and influence form, but the relationship between the two is often treated as a one-way street. In academia and theory, this relationship is treated more fluidly. It is a fairly common occurrence for the jury of a student's final review to devote equal time to both the program and aesthetics of a project. Practicing architects who either teach or lecture generally seem more amenable to attempting to affect program as well, but for the most part, professionals are happy enough to leave questions of program alone. This indifference is often justified with some permutation of the argument

[1]
George Wittkowsky, "Swift's Modest Proposal: The Biography of an Early Georgian Pamphlet." *Journal of the History of Ideas* 4, no. 1 (1943): 75-104.

that dictating program is the purview of the client alone. And indeed, in many instances, this is largely true. Often, the only recourse an architect would have to meaningfully alter the intended program of a space is to threaten to walk from the project unless change is affected. Refusing a project on moral grounds is rarely suggested in our field; indeed, many architects would be more willing to advocate walking away from a project because of client interference in its design and aesthetics before they would suggest the same due to moral implications. Architects would be more incentivized to refuse a project on ethical grounds if they felt that not doing so would subject them to sufficient cultural and institutional censure. So what then is the current state of institutional pressure on architects?

On January 6, 2015, the AIA rejected a proposal brought forward by a group of its members to update its Code of Ethics to explicitly censure members who design solitary confinement cells or death chambers. Former AIA president Helene Combs Dreiling said of the decision, "it's just not something we want to determine as a collective. Members with deeply embedded beliefs will avoid designing those building types and leave it to their colleagues. Architects self-select, depending on where they feel they can contribute best."[2] Why doesn't the AIA feel that it is justified in censuring the design of death chambers? The reality is, had the AIA committed itself to drawing a moral line here, they would have opened the door to further questions of morality in our work. Is any project that is not carbon-neutral morally egregious? What about high-end residential projects, which have increasingly become a means by which the ultra-rich store away wealth, further widening economic inequality? Do architects have an obligation to refuse to design the sorts of tech campuses Google and Facebook have built at the expense of the adjacent local populations?

Defining the ethical boundaries of architecture and holding each other to a moral standard is going to be tough, and it's going to require our field to answer many questions we would rather leave unasked. Our industry has been able to avoid these sorts of hard questions because of the perceived lack of a cohesive ethic pertaining to the field. But much like the circumstances of Swift's contemporaries, the inability to perceive a theoretical framework does not imply the lack of one. All architecture, from the shed to the stadium, is bounded by a framework. Satire, such as Swift's *A Modest Proposal*, can be used to reveal a set of previously unacknowledged beliefs, and to begin a conversation around them. The satire I present in *A Modest Request For Proposals* demonstrates that these boundaries do exist: no firm would genuinely accept Swift Food's commission. The question is, as we continue to define these boundaries, are we going to like where they are? 🐇

2
Michael Kimmelman, "Prison Architecture and the Question of Ethics," *New York Times*, February 16, 2015.

The State of Things is Very Serious.

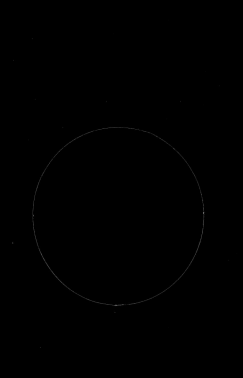

From Martha Warren Beckwith, "Eating Tiger's Guts," in *Jamaica Anansi Tales* (New York: The American Folklore Society, 1924).

"Brer Tiger and Brer Anansi went to river-side. Brer Anansi said, 'Brer Tiger, tak out your inside an' wash it out.' Brer Tiger did so. 'Now, Brer Tiger, dip your head in water wash it good.' The moment Brer Tiger put his head in water, Anansi took up the inside and run away with it to give to his wife Tacoomah to boil."

Knotty Trees

Jenna Dezinski and John Paul Rysavy | And-Either-Or

Knotty Trees responds to a prompt for an event space on a former tree farm in central West Michigan. Nominally spaced four feet on center in rows six feet apart, black hill pine and blue spruce trees outgrew their intention as a nursery for domestic landscaping and Christmas trees. Amid the undergrowth, the project seeks to spatialize the event through dematerialized figuration. A rectangle and triangle of the same 30-60-90 primitive shape are arranged axially about their shared symmetry, joined by an extended aisle, juxtaposing casual and formal assemblies. Transcribed by absence, each dim figure invites eventuality through the perceived delineation of trimmed and knotted branches, a suspended canopy, and floor of pine needles. The project interrogates architecture's origins by considering the primitive and challenging institutional lines between building and landscape, idea and construct.

Through its uncovering, *Knotty Trees* upends conventional delimitations of architecture. The project exposes the underside—a cross-section of knots—inverting traditional precepts of architecture as a construct. From the normative inflection of a building's inception, the project achieves its full spatiality through excavation. Its bounds, however, are immaterial. *Knotty Trees* disrobes architecture of its conventional covering—customarily defined by layered assemblies—leaving the empirical without any clothes. While modern construction celebrates a glossy, lustrous, and synthetic materiality, *Knotty Trees* strips the perceived constitution of an enclosure, delineating interiority by a low-resolution pointillism of

trimmed limbs and skewed branches. Rather than exert domination over a found nature, *Knotty Trees* exploits its unruly, undisciplined essence.

Not quite architecture, yet nonetheless architectural, the resultant construct is an ephemeral event—materialized by the passing of wind, dappling of sun, scattering of leaves, crickets, and birds, organized by a repetitive colonnade of knotted trunks and point cloud enclosure; a form akin to the archetypal hypostyle hall, catacombs, ambulacra and cryptae, pleached hedge, and arboreal bocage. Through the subversive and disorderly, *Knotty Trees* suggests that architecture as a primitive practice is, first and foremost, a conceptual act; a spatial event. By bending the rules, or in this case, the branches, *Knotty Trees* demonstrates an expanded platform of consequence and opportunity for the design disciplines to consider. 🐇

fig. 2
Detail of Rectangle Hall Axon

fig. 3 (facing)
Rectangle Hall Axon and Triangle Hall Axon

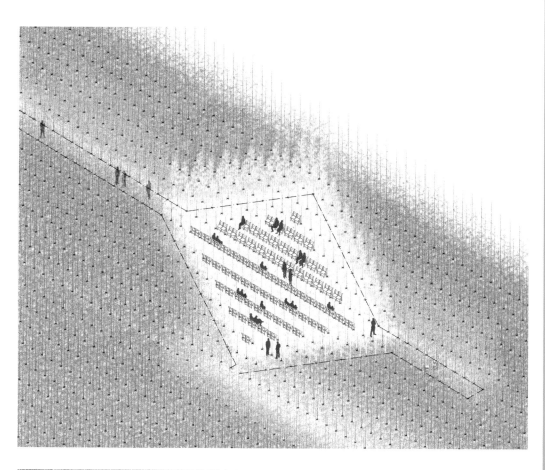
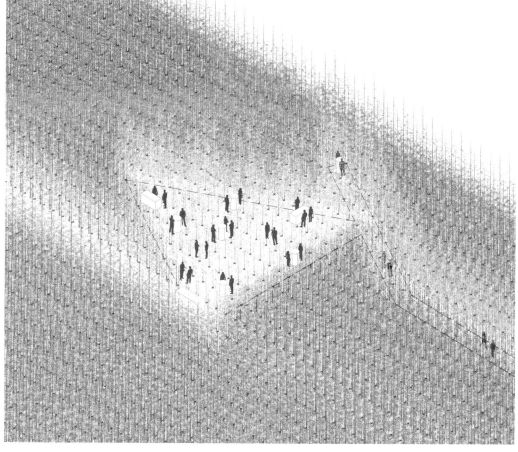

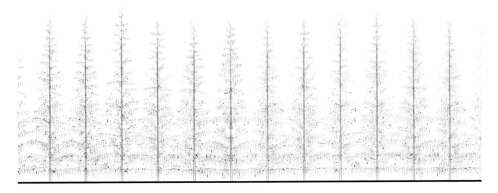

Existing

Great Aisle

Rectangle Hall

fig. 4 (above)
Site Sections

fig. 5 (facing)
Entry to the Rectangle Hall
(Photo: John Paul Rysavy)

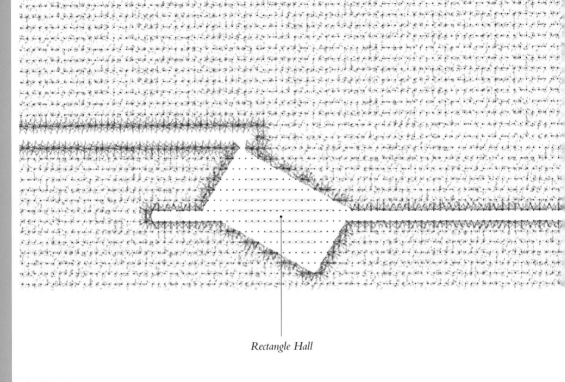

Rectangle Hall

fig. 6 (above)
Knotty Trees Plan

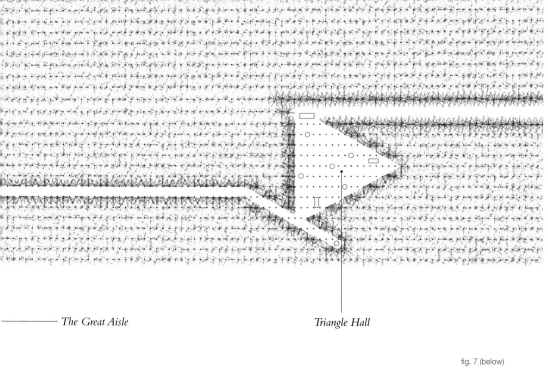

The Great Aisle   _Triangle Hall_

fig. 7 (below)
Knotty Trees Canopy
(Photo: Sam Pepper)

The Trouble with Alaska

Katie Kelly and Anna Morrison

1

John McPhee, *Coming into the
Country* (New York: Bantam, 1981),
18.

From the outside looking in, Alaska has been characterized by any number of terms and categories: *arctic, wild, frozen waste.* The trouble with Alaska is that it cannot be defined simply. "The central paradox of Alaska," as John McPhee wrote, "is that it is as small as it is large—an immense landscape with so few people in it that language is stretched to call it a frontier, let alone a state."[1] This vastness creates space for contradictions, which, like cracks in pavement, spread wider with each freeze and thaw until, like the potholes in every Alaskan road, they become too large to veer around.

As its native people were collectively labelled "Native Alaskan" despite their differing languages and ways of life, the Alaskan landscape itself has been treated as one simple tract of land. Far from it. Place your hand in front of your face and you will find, perhaps to your surprise, that they are the same size. Do the same with Alaska and the "lower 48" and you will find that it would cover an entire fifth of the US, making it three times larger than Texas. (Alaskans like to mention this with an air of pity.) This land, defined by boundaries indifferent to the waters, contours, or people they cross, leads one to question at what scale Alaska can be understood, and what effect statewide policies have had on the diverse land they govern.

Over 12,000 years ago, the Bering Land Bridge allowed the Tlingit people to cross into Alaska from Siberia. In the 2,000 years that followed, the Athabaskan, Aleut, and Eskimo people settled parts of the

Alaskan and Canadian territories. Settlement was dictated by latitude and the geographic features and resources that made a place more or less habitable. "Habitable" is, of course, a relative term. Indigenous communities defied modern expectations of human survival, developing a culture based on resourcefulness and subsistence. These communities, still in existence today, have lived through the invention of writing, agriculture, and the rise and fall of the Roman Empire—not to mention the end of the Ice Age. Native cultures have changed and hybridized continuously in response to shifting climates and social encounters for thousands of years.

Nevertheless, the political and economic changes resulting from mid-twentieth-century colonialism have rapidly altered native cultural and spatial practices as well as the Alaskan landscape itself. The accelerating climatic changes impacting Alaska portend an equally dramatic effect, as melting sea ice inundates coastal communities and food sources move or die out.[2]

The following sections are reflections on perceived facets of Alaska: *nomad, oil, whale, cold, native.* By focusing on the complexity of these often simplified features, this essay explores how contemporary Alaska defies expectation. The trouble with Alaska is that it cannot be easily defined.

It is through generalization and specificity, through aerial photos and ground-level observations, that Alaska is created, and thus it must be understood. This essay weaves between secondary-source understandings of Alaska and firsthand travel experiences of a 10-day trip undertaken as part of the Arctic Design Studio at the University of Virginia.[3] Traversing scales, like a camera lens struggling to focus, forces one to choose between foreground and background, haptic and optic. By zooming in and out, by privileging the haptic and optic in turn, our lens may begin to focus.

I. Cold

Perhaps one of the greatest misconceptions of Alaska is that it is cold. It is cold sometimes and in some places, but not in the times and places it is thought to be—always and everywhere.

We began in Anchorage—"about 30 minutes from Alaska," as they say. The weather in mid-October was cool and rainy, buffered by its proximity to the Alaskan Gulf. The roads were much wider than the traffic moving along them, for snow removal—two lanes for cars, two for snow. As we moved north, the evidence of cold became more obvious, as vegetation shrunk and infrastructure started rising out of the ground to avoid permafrost. On our last leg of the trip we arrived in Utqiagvik, formerly known as Barrow, the northernmost city in the United States, in the midst of a blizzard. We descended into the treeless frozen marsh to find a city adapted to cold as a way of life (fig. 2). Out of buildings sprout blue electrical plugs that are used to keep cars warm enough while they are parked so they will turn on again. The city's sewage system runs above ground through pipes around eye height.

2

Alaska is warming two times faster than the national US average. F. Stuart Chapin and Sarah F. Trainor, National Climate Assessment, nca2014.globalchange.gov/report/regions/alaska.

3

The Arctic Design Studio and trip were sponsored by the Arctic Design Group, University of Virginia, Center for Global Inquiry and Innovation, and the Anchorage Museum.

4

The Alaska National Wildlife
Refuge—recently opened for oil
drilling—sits within the eastern
portion of the Brooks Range.

Utqiagvik is the largest city in the North Slope "borough," cut off from the rest of the state by the Brooks Range.[4] The term "borough" seems ill-fitting given that it encompasses 95,000 square miles, making it nearly 3,000 times the size of the borough of Manhattan and the largest borough governed by one mayor in the country. The North Slope, encompassing the northern quarter of the state (more than twice the area of Virginia), is the region of Alaska that sits within the Arctic Circle, where permafrost is continuous and trees do not grow. Oddly enough, this area does not see temperatures as extreme as interior Alaska, which can swing from -80°F to 100°F over the year. Permafrost is discontinuous in interior Alaska.

Cold takes many forms. In the North Slope, the frozen ground serves as the foundations of buildings. Like igneous bedrock, permafrost requires a power tool or a very persistent axe to drill into it. It is a strong foundation, but its integrity requires consistently frozen ground, and all measures are taken to ensure the ground does not melt and take the building with it. To keep permafrost frozen, structures are lifted on stilts, buffering the heat produced by building systems and human life from the surface of the ground.

Regardless of how high the building is lofted, the ground is in constant flux due to the freezing and thawing of the active layer, and buildings often need to be moved. Cutting-edge building technology in arctic Alaska involves installing hydraulic lifts under buildings to jack them up when they inevitably sink. Leading engineers have built houses on skis so that they can be easily moved. Others have installed thermal extraction systems under buildings so that they can create their own permafrost.

5

An Athabaskan town located 100
miles northwest of Fairbanks.
There are 11 distinct Athabaskan
languages.

In interior Alaska, the coldness of the ground can be read in the patterns of the landscape (fig. 3). The Native Alaskan village of Minto[5] is situated between the Minto river flats and the forest, in the frozen patch of ground between the unfrozen water and the unfrozen ground where black spruce and aspens can grow. This position is thermally strategic and rich in resources. The flats provide fish when they freeze over, bridging the town to a series of forested islands. The forest provides moose, berries, and other food sources that ebb and flow with the seasons. Athabaskan culture is built around these changes, moving with and celebrating the cold.

The shifting of global climate patterns poses a more permanent threat to coldness in Far North Alaska. Early signs of climate change have been seen in the warming Arctic Ocean, melting sea ice and intensifying the incoming waves, breaching sea walls and eroding towns. Native game and fowl are changing their migration patterns, leaving their hunters behind. Towns built on permafrost are moving buildings to shrinking pockets of frozen ground. Underground ice cellars carved into the permafrost are caving in.[6]

6

At the Inupiat Heritage Center in
Barrow it was relayed to us that
these ice cellars have been passed
down for generations.

At the same time, parts of Alaska are becoming more habitable. The cold once prevented certain degrees of development and industry in Alaska. There is very little agriculture in the state and frozen channels prevent

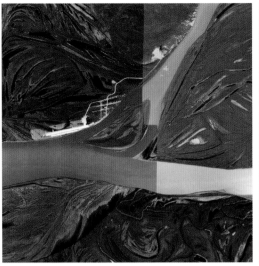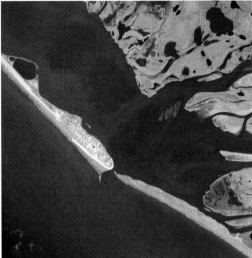

major shipping routes. But warming is opening the state to speculation, and change is imminent.

II. Nomad

> *"The opposition between the striated and the smooth is not simply that of the global and the local. For in one case, the global is still relative, whereas in the other the local is already absolute. Where there is close vision, space is not visual, or rather the eye itself has a haptic, non-optical function: no line separates earth from sky, which are of the same substance; there is neither horizon nor background nor perspective nor limit nor outline or form nor center, there is no intermediary distance, or all distance is intermediary. Like Eskimo space."* [7]

Over the span of four days in Utqiagvik, the ground changed daily. The first day, we weren't sure what it was made of. The streets, the yards, and the beach all looked the same. On the second day, we photographed stuff we found on the ground. There isn't a better word for it than "stuff." Sometimes it was stuff in use, like a freezer or a basketball; other times it was clearly discarded. The third day it snowed and every step was a gamble that your foot wouldn't land in a semi-frozen puddle or a trench. On the fourth day, they used part of the road to bolster the sea wall and a backhoe redirected traffic along the lake.

The status of movement in Alaska depends on your frame of reference. As recently as the 1960s, Native Alaskan communities lived nomadically, in smooth space *par excellence*. Movement and settlement followed seasonal patterns of animal migration, ground conditions, and trading opportunities, as well as shifts in technology and opportunity. The invention of the kayak, for example, opened up hunting in broken sea ice conditions for the Aleut, Inuit, and Yupik people, extending the hunting season to new times and places.[8]

To say that the nomadic landscape was smooth is not to say that it was even or homogeneous or easy to move across. Geographical features like the Brooks Range, the Yukon River, and patterned ice wedge polygons

fig. 2 (previous spread)
Children playing in the Alaskan alley, a wide space between houses where spare things are stored and snowmobiles travel through in the winter

7
Gilles Deleuze and Felix Guattari, *A Thousand Plateaus: Capitalism and Schizophrenia*. (Minneapolis: University of Minnesota Press, 1987), 494

8
"Alaska Native Subsistence: A Matter of Cultural Survival" in *Cultural Survival*, Sept. 1998, www.culturalsurvival.org/publications/cultural-survival-quarterly/alaska-native-subsistence-matter-cultural-survival.

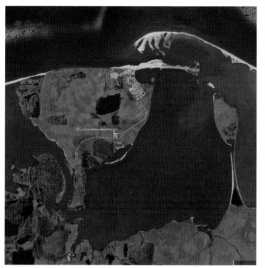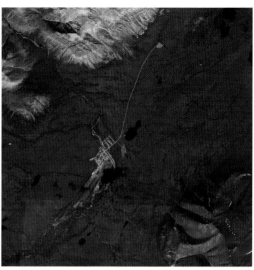

fig. 3 (facing and above)
Remote Alaskan villages are most
often not connected to a statewide
road network. Instead, they rely on
airports which are attached via a
long gravel road to each town.

form folds in the landscape, but not borders. Nomadic movement chafed against the parceling of land that came with statehood in 1959. A divisive land claim settlement between the federal government and native tribes created a striated landscape of order and control, in which Alaskans were organized into "corporations" and asked to choose permanent settlement locations. Populations defined by their mobility suddenly became static.

These settlements established a new relationship of human movement to landscape, one of distance and coordinates, where the landscape is a liability, its richness and dynamic qualities at odds with movement across it. The frequent freezing and thawing of the active layer cracks and warps any surface adhered to it, making a statewide road network an impossibility. As of 2018, 82% of Alaskan communities are not served by roads. Instead, a tributary aviation network is the primary mode of travel across the state, wherein every remote community has an airport, a long unpaved road, and then a town.

Food and goods are brought in by barge or air shipments a few times a year, depending on location. The expense of the lengthy supply chain drives up the costs of purchasing outside goods, such as milk, vegetables, and TVs. The cost of removing them from town is rarely justified, so underperforming refrigerators and broken cars accumulate in junkyards and the area surrounding homes. Like animal carcasses, which up north can take years to decompose due to the preserving force of the polar climate, material possessions linger beyond their useful life.

Seen from the state scale, Alaskan villages are clumped, feebly attached to flows of people and goods, and therefore littered with waste. Zoom in, however, and you will find fluidity of movement. The backhoe may drive at a new angle one day creating a new street network altogether. Snowmobiles (known as "snow machines") open up new networks of movement in the winter when residents can navigate the open land between houses and boats and piles of stuff. It is here where the striated yields to the smooth, where stuff is again an event in the landscape, and human movement is limited by folds, not borders (fig. 4).

fig. 4 (above and facing)
Roadside images of the changing
landscape along the Elliott highway
en route to Minto.

III. Oil

The pipe snaked along to the left of the Elliott Highway—one of only a handful of main roads in Alaska—lofted above ground on ten-foot-high pilings until it disappeared underground briefly, reappearing in and out of sight on our left side, asserting itself within the scrappy black spruce taiga. At a pull-over just north of Fairbanks, we stopped our trucks to get a closer look. A short gravel path and a small bridge over a stream led us into the presence of the thing that for a hundred miles had been playing a game of hide-and-seek out the passenger window. The pipeline stood there in front of us, like an animal at the zoo, replete with a board of information and statistics and the opportunity to stand next to it, under it even, for photos. The belly of the pipe was unreachable by even the tallest person, and its physical presence ranked somewhere between disturbing and majestic.

The manifestations of policies impact almost every facet of Alaskan life, enacted upon a culture and landscape seemingly indifferent to policy. Notions of ownership and boundaries were introduced to the new state of Alaska and its inhabitants in the early 20th century, until the state was wholly sliced and adjudicated. This notion of ownership, the drawing of lines on the landscape, once ran counter to Native Alaskan cultures: as John McPhee wrote, "[River Eskimos] see a river not as an entity but as a pageant of parts, and every bend and eddy has a name."[9] Where Native Alaskans once used resource availability and climate patterns to define their boundaries, static physical and political barriers now serve as uneasy anchors.

9
McPhee, *Coming into the Country.*
Bantam, 24.

The Trans-Alaska Pipeline System (TAPS), stretching the length of the eastern middle of the state, runs north to south like a crooked spine. After the demand for oil created by the 1973 oil crisis made drilling in Prudhoe Bay viable, scientists began collecting exhaustive physiographic and geologic data to map out the ideal path for the pipe. Through air-photo analysis, a careful path for the 800-mile pipe was chosen. This path crosses 13 physiographic units and three mountain

10
R.A. Kreig and R.D. Reger, "Air-
photo analysis and summary of
landform soil properties along
the route of the trans-Alaska
pipeline system," *Alaska Division
of Geological & Geophysical
Surveys Geologic Report* 66 (1982),
doi:10.14509/426.

11
Ibid.

12
Ibid.

13
Ibid.

14
"U.S. Census Bureau QuickFacts:
Alaska," Census Bureau QuickFacts,
2010, www.census.gov/quickfacts/
AK.

15
A neighborhood in Utqiagvik named
after the National Atmospheric
Research Laboratory,

ranges.[10] It traverses the Tiekel, Yukon, Lowe, and Tanana River valleys, passing through starkly differentiated landscapes from the "complexly folded and faulted Cretaceous graywacke, phyllite and greenstone,"[11] to the "rounded, stream-dissected hills and ridges of late Paleozoic pelitic schist."[12] It crosses approximately 600 miles of permafrost and, at its highest elevation, reaches nearly 5,000 feet above sea level.[13] While aerial imagery helped to site the pipeline, the spatial implications of this surgical industrial insertion into the landscape can only be felt up close, under the belly of the beast.

An aerial view of the pipeline obscures the effects it has had socially, culturally, and economically (fig. 5 and 6). Pipeline-related construction and maintenance jobs, for example, were the impetus for a mass migration of men across the country, creating the highest ratio of males to females in the country. While this ratio is not significant at the state scale, Prudhoe Bay, the "headwater" of the pipeline, is 90% male.[14] Having exceeded its 30-year lifespan and with dwindling oil production, the pipeline's physical and economic decline poses a threat to local populations.

The central spatial dilemma of Alaska is that of scale. Staring at an aerial of the pipeline and standing beneath it sharpens McPhee's insight that Alaska is "as small as it is large."

IV. Whale

"Come out to NARL[15] area. Ask taxi driver to take you to whale." This was the text message we received mere hours before we were scheduled to leave Utqiagvik. Fall whaling season had begun only three days prior, delayed by a blizzard—the storm that greeted us upon our arrival to the Inupiaq town—and we were told not to get our hopes up about a whale any time soon. We called a Polar Cab—a cab service with only one competitor, Arctic Cab—and within ten minutes we were on our way to witness the whale. Our cab drove cautiously down a wide dirt road laden with deep potholes as locals in trucks raced past us. The road's

broad shoulder served as kind of whale graveyard, lined with bowhead whale skulls from previous whaling seasons. When we arrived thoroughly rattled after a bumpy 15 minutes, the whale—shiny and wet, with steam rising off its body—was there before us, surrounded by several hundred onlookers and participants.

Before oil was a desirable resource, whales dominated the subsistence economy of coastal Native Alaskans. In Inupiaq communities, whales persist as a central cultural, economic, and political force. Though the Inupiaq people have been limited in the number of whales they can catch per season,[16] it remains a major source of wealth for the city.[17]

The socio-ecological entanglement of humans and nature is exemplified in the whale's spatial and material significance in modern Inupiaq culture. Whaling families, many of them descendants of the nineteenth-century European whaling captain Charles Brower, remain some of the most politically active and powerful people in the Utqiagvik community. One of the three neighborhoods in Utqiagvik is named Browerville, and the recent mayoral election pitted Browers against Browers. Whalers served as the original community leaders, providing maktak[18] from the first whale of the season to every family in the community, a practice that still persists today. It is not surprising that this role has been translated and hybridized for the contemporary political frame.

The hybridization of modern materials with native cultural practices has made Native Alaskans incredibly resilient. Transportation costs and protectionist policies[19] have made seemingly ordinary goods prohibitively expensive: a gallon of milk at the grocery store costs $10. Though this has had detrimental effects on remote Alaskans' ability to afford fuel and other necessities, it has insulated their economy from some of the cultural depletion of global capitalism. Though Native Alaskans have traded their *yugluqtaak*[20] for plastic sunglasses, cultural practices connected to the landscape are still vital to communities. Subsistence is not only a question of cultural preservation in Utqiagvik. It is necessary and changing; ancient but alive—not unlike the whales themselves.

V. Native

We drove along the Elliot Highway to Minto, one of the few native villages accessible by road. At lunch with the elders I sat with a man named Frederick who was friendly but understandably distant, skeptical of a group of architecture students from "the lower 48" visiting his town for only a few hours. They served us salmon chowder, and I cautiously tongued for bones, following Frederick's lead, watching him casually remove bones as he ate and placing them on his plate. The soup was delicious and I proclaimed this more times than was necessary to fill the silences between us. He was recently retired, he said, after 30 years as a firefighter.

"This soup is delicious," I said again. "Do you like to fish?" I asked, looking over Frederick's shoulder and out the window to the Minto flats, a series of rivers spilling out into the valley where nomadic Athabaskan

---

16
The International Whaling Commission has limited Utqiagvik to twenty-four whales per year, though the community has argued for a higher quota.

17
The inequities of these strict environmental policies in contrast to the historically lax restrictions on oil extraction should not go unquestioned.

18
The traditional meal of frozen whale skin and blubber.

19
The Merchant Marine Act of 1920 has had drastic economic implications for all of Alaska, forcing foreign goods to pass first through Seattle, driving up the cost of everything from building materials to groceries and clothing.

20
Carved wooden snow goggles used by Native Alaskan hunters to protect their eyes from bright snow.

people used to travel in the warm season to fish. "There aren't any salmon here," he said. "You have to travel north some ways to find the salmon. They used to be bigger you know. They caught all the big salmon and now they are much smaller." This was the general theme of our conversation. Immense loss seemed to fill all the spaces between his words.

Within the classification of "Native Alaskan" there are eleven distinct cultures and 26 languages, and still more dialects within those languages. What was once a collection of many discrete cultures has become an amalgam of rituals and languages, united by a deep yet multiplicitous understanding of place. Survival through economic deprivation, ecological devastation, and cultural dismantling has made Native Alaskans incredibly resilient people. Contemporary Native Alaskans do not reject modernization; rather, they have been denied the opportunity to adopt Western practices on their own terms.

The simultaneous cleansing of culture and landscape—beginning slowly in the nineteenth century and peaking in the mid-twentieth century with the forced displacement of Native Alaskan children from their villages— has left communities straddling two worlds, before and after statehood. In fact, most elders born before the 1950s were raised in a nomadic, subsistence lifestyle, transitioning to "contemporary" life within less than a lifetime (fig. 7). The tension between old and new, we were told, is something that Native Alaskan people have to regularly confront.

The history of this tension is that people had to choose. To reject one's culture and integrate into a foreign one was a choice so painful it has permeated generations of families, made manifest in a cascade of suicides and substance abuse from which communities have not recovered.[21] A hybrid culture has grown out of this trauma, one that defies the expectations of outsiders. Despite the significant loss of tradition, language, and land, Native Alaskan culture persists in the materials and spatial practices of its people. Native Alaskans are people residing within two places, one a distant-yet-proximate memory and the other a distant-yet-proximate present.

On the way out of Minto we stopped at the village cemetery. The site was on a moderate slope, the plots not following much of a grid. There was no manicured lawn, only dense soil thinly covered in shin-high grasses and optimistic saplings. An aspen and spruce forest framed the cemetery on three sides. Each grave was marked with a simple cross constructed of two boards; some were painted a color, others were bare wood. All were marked with names and the date of birth and death. Alexander, Titus, Charlie: all the common last names that we had seen on the community bulletin board were clustered together by family.

The most ornate plots were completely enclosed by white picket fence and embellished with bouquets of fake flowers. I was struck by this: symbols of the suburban American landscape had found their way to even the most remote areas of Alaska. My grandma would plant fake flowers at her husband's grave—water them even—and at the mausoleums in

fig. 6 (facing)
Notes taken during a meeting with the former North Slope mayors, Charlotte Brower and her husband Eugene Brower.

21
Most Native Alaskan villages are dry, meaning that alcohol and drugs are not permitted in the townships because of the prevalence of substance abuse and domestic violence.

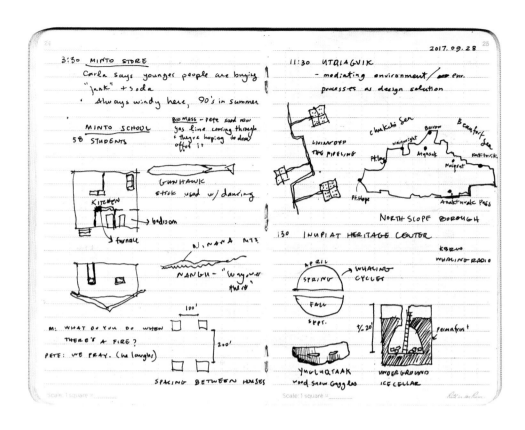

24

3:30 MINTO STORE

Carla says younger people are buying "junk" + soda
- Always windy here, 90's in summer

MINTO SCHOOL
58 STUDENTS

BIOMASS - Pete said new gas line coming through + they're hoping to draw off it

GUN HAWK stick used w/ dancing

KITCHEN
→ bedroom
→ furnace

NINANA MTS

NANBU - "way over there"

M: WHAT DO YOU DO WHEN THERE'S A FIRE?

PETE: WE PRAY. (he laughs)

100'
200'

SPACING BETWEEN HOUSES

Scale: 1 square = _____

11:30 UTQIAGVIK
- mediating environment / env. processes as design solution

Chukchi Sea   Barrow   Beaufort Sea
LIVENGOOD   Wainwright   Kaktovik
THE PIPELINE   Pt. Lay   Atqasuk   Nuiqsut
Pt. Hope   Anaktuvuk Pass

NORTH SLOPE BOROUGH

1:30 INUPIAT HERITAGE CENTER

KBRW WHALING RADIO

APRIL
SPRING   WHALING CYCLES
FALL
SEPT.

1/20

permafrost

yngluqtaak wood snow goggles

UNDERGROUND ICE CELLAR

Scale: 1 square = _____

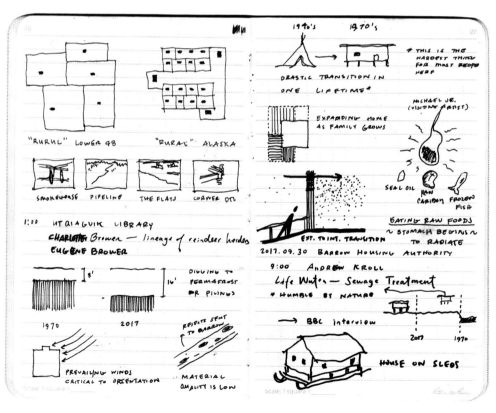

86

"RURAL" LOWER 48   "RURAL" ALASKA

SMOKEHOUSE   PIPELINE   THE FLATS   CORNER DTL

1:00 UTQIAGVIK LIBRARY

CHARLOTTE Brower — lineage of reindeer herders
EUGENE BROWER

8'   16'   DIGGING TO PERMAFROST OR PILINGS

1970   2017

REFLECTS SENT TO BARROW

PREVAILING WINDS CRITICAL TO ORIENTATION

MATERIAL QUALITY IS LOW

Scale: 1 square = _____

1940's   1970's

DRASTIC TRANSITION IN ONE LIFETIME*

* THIS IS THE HARDEST THING FOR MOST PEOPLE HERE

EXPANDING HOME AS FAMILY GROWS

MICHAEL JR. (VISITING ARTIST)

SEAL OIL   RAW CARIBOU   FROZEN FISH

EATING RAW FOODS
~ STOMACH BEGINS TO RADIATE ~

EXT. POINT. TRANSITION

2017.09.30 BARROW HOUSING AUTHORITY

9:00 ANDREW KROLL
Life Water — Sewage Treatment
* HUMBLE BY NATURE

→ BBC interview

2017   1970

HOUSE ON SLEDS

Scale: 1 square = _____

Venice, the graves stacked three meters high as far as one could see, each small plaque had an equally small vase filled with polyester flowers. I thought of these distant sites, of the human instinct to memorialize the dead, which spans states and continents, and of the practicality of plastic flowers. We walked back in silence. "The graves are facing south," my friend said, "towards the sun." 🐇

PARTY TIME!

Tear this page up, rip it out, festively scatter it all about.

Woof

Evan Pavka

How do you know if someone is an architect? They'll tell you. When perusing profiles on a dating app, how do you know if someone is an architect? They'll tell you: fountain pen, straight ruler, set square, office building emoji.

Dating apps play an ever-growing role in the social spaces of the contemporary world, yet their relationship to architecture at large has been barely mined. From Tinder and OkCupid to Grindr and Scruff, the implications of these virtual social spaces increasingly play out in very real material places. They sexualize ordinary life, provide new kinds of intersubjectivity, and extend far beyond the frame of a smart phone screen.[1]

1
See Andres Jacque, "Grindr Archiurbanism," *LOG* 41 (2017): 74-84.

Where cities, saunas, homes, and sex clubs once provided the few places where non-heterosexual identities could be expressed, dating and hook-up apps have embedded every space with erotic potential. Though historically rooted in technologies of geolocation and surveillance, can the subversive use of dating apps to create novel digital relationships offer us potential modes of anti-capitalist engagement with which to counter the power structures inherent in the architecture profession?

While dating apps saturate the contemporary world, they have a much deeper history interwoven with the expansion of digital media and its effect on hetero- and homo-social relations. In 1965, two Harvard undergraduate students, Jeff Tarr and Vaughan Morrill, developed the

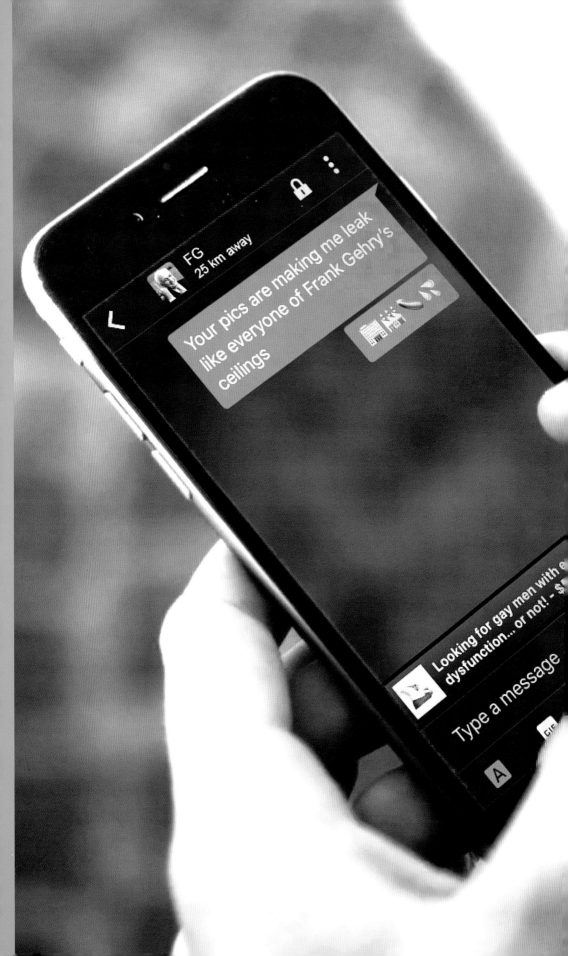

2

Dan Slater, *Love in the Time of Algorithms: What Technology Does to Meeting and Mating* (New York: Current, 2013), 16-20.

first modern dating app: Operation Match. Running on an IBM 1401—one of the earliest mass-market computers—Operation Match analyzed paper questionnaires copied onto punch cards to match co-eds with five romantic potentials in mere seconds.[2]

By the early 2000s, almost every home across North America was equipped with a personal computer. The first decade of the 21st century saw the rapid expansion of online dating with the release of the dating service eHarmony in the summer of 2000, followed by Manhunt in the spring of 2001. Additional services like Plenty of Fish and OkCupid—launched in 2003 and 2004, respectively—rounded out the selection of hetero- and homo-social services. A year after smart phones entered the global market in 2008, the location-based queer, trans-, and bi- app Grindr launched. This was soon followed by Scruff in 2010.

Scruff, founded by Eric Silverberg and John Skandros, employs geospatial technology to provide users with both a local and global grid of active users. After completing a pre-set questionnaire outlining physical traits, location, interests (both in and out of bed), and what you are "looking for" (chat, dates, relationship, NSA or Right Now, among others), the profile is uploaded to the sea of more than 12 million users. In addition to providing a list of active members in one's immediate vicinity, the app provides grids of users across the globe alongside new and popular profiles.

3

These labels, though attributed to intercourse between men, were informed by heterosexual pairings. The term "fairie" generally connoted men who violated gender conventions, rather than simply engaged in homosexual practices, while also attributed to flamboyantly effeminate males. The term "trade" was used to describe men, usually of the working class, who would engage in relations with "fairies," yet did not diverge from "normal" masculinity. Terms such as "wolves," "husbands," and "jockers," denoted men who abided by conventions of masculinity, similar to "trades," but preferred male sex partners. George Chauncey, *Gay New York: Gender, Urban Culture, and the Making of the Gay Male World 1890 - 1940* (New York: Basic Books, 1994), 67-68, 97; See also George Chauncey, "Christian Brotherhood or Sexual Perversion? Homosexual Identities and the Construction of Sexual Boundaries in the World War One Era," *Journal of Social History* 19, no. 2 (1985): 205.

Playing on the animal lexicons used to define queer sub-communities—Otters, Bears, Wolves, and so on—Scruff provides an in-app message akin to a Facebook Poke: a Woof.[3] A "Woof" primarily signals that one user finds the other attractive. The message is commonly employed as a method of garnering attention without the potential rejection a more direct message offers, whether the profile is 200 feet or 2,000 miles away.

It is therefore not uncommon for an app user to view their notifications and discover that a series of Woofs has been sent their way. Upon checking my own notifications on one particular day, I scanned the selection of international profiles ranging from 4,000 to 6,000 miles away only to find that one came from someone much closer.

Upon opening the profile, I realized the user who had messaged me was, in fact, a prominent member of Toronto's architectural community. Playing along, I decided to engage in a conversation. After swapping pleasantries and fetishes, the conversation veered toward occupation. While my answer was deliberately obtuse, opting simply for "freelance writer," it only took him moments to confirm his occupation: architect.

What followed, on my part, was a deliberate act of trolling. Urban Dictionary tells us trolling is "the art of deliberately, cleverly, and secretly pissing people off, usually via the Internet, using dialogue."[4] And that is exactly what unfolded. Pressing the topic, I inquired as to what projects he was currently involved with. Rattling off a selection of articles, exhibitions, and the like, the conversation quickly shifted from intros to academic interests. Each project he mentioned was met with a response—from questions on theoretical frameworks and logical fallacies to further reading on complex subjects seemingly reduced to shallow premises. The "Woof" signaled the beginning of a playful dialogue that quickly led from introductions to a deep discussion of his current work, of which I was able to offer blunt criticism without fear of institutional recourse.

He appeared taken aback at first—perhaps even uncomfortable—about an unfamiliar kind of criticism emerging from an unexpected place. "Trolling requires deceiving," says Urban Dictionary. "Any trolling that doesn't involve deceiving someone isn't trolling at all."[5] Our hour-long conversation unfolded without a clear confirmation of each other's names, until my commentary had exasperated him to the point that he simply responded, "You're mean."

Though more commonly used to describe the activities of those intent on propagating white hetero-patriarchal ideology, trolling is one strategy for operating outside of the institutionalized debates within the architecture profession. These institutions arguably propagate similarly suppressive forces, as evident in a recent survey by the *Architects' Journal*. The survey found that UK-based LGBTTI2QQA architects still fear their sexuality may prevent access to certain career paths and thus only 73% report being "out."[6] The article and its publication on other platforms such as *Dezeen* drew the attention of active architecture trolls such as Steve Florida, whose bigoted comments on articles from *ArchDaily* to *Catholic Authenticity* further reinforce the threats faced by queer people in digital spaces.[7] Operating beyond the borders of heteronormative academia, professionalism, and digital comment sections, where queerness is often cast as a commodity or potential conflict, non-heterosexual dating apps like Scruff flatten sexuality, desire, and criticism into a space where trolling can be generative.

Given the digital platform that supported our dialogue, perhaps the most fascinating part of our exchange was his continued engagement with me on the subject of his work. While the framework for traditional institutional criticism is ultimately influenced by social, economic, and political factors, the driving force behind apps like Scruff is desire. In a study of Grindr users, Rusi Jaspal articulates how desire not only informs communication, but also the construction of online identities. "Grindr reportedly allowed its users to present a particular desire to other users and to construct an identity consistent with this desire," argues Jaspal.[8] Within the space of the dating app, desire is currency—perhaps the most important currency.

By inhabiting a space where desire and not capital was a fundamental driver, the app allowed for a kind of confrontational trolling rarely allowed within the rigid hierarchies of the architecture profession. Academia, exhibitions, conferences, publications, and organized debates have provided controlled environments for architectural criticism to circulate.[9] While academic and professional power is woven into networks of notoriety, the instant gratification of apps counters these capitalist professional protocols. Safety and vulnerability are negotiated

4
"Trolling," Urban Dictionary, September 21, 2009, accessed February 17, 2018, https://www.urbandictionary.com/define.php?term=Trolling.

5
Ibid.

6
Richard Waite, "The AJ's LGBT+ survey 'reflects a less tolerant society,'" *Architects' Journal*, January 26, 2018, https://www.architectsjournal.co.uk/news/the-ajs-lgbt-survey-reflects-a-less-tolerant-society/10027332.article.

7
Username Steve Florida has said homophobia was "coined by active homosexuals as a defence mechanism" and has also touted a misogynistic understanding of gender stating the following about President Donald Trump's attempted ban on openly trans members of the military: "This whole TG thing in the military is absolutely disgusting. Can you image the Generals of WWII tolerating 'soldiers' prancing around in red high heels? It just makes me want to vomit." Ironically, he has also posted commentary below articles I have written for *ArchDaily*.

8
Rusi Jaspal, "Gay Men's Construction and Management of Identity on Grindr," *Sexuality & Culture* 21 (2017): 194.

within the space of the app—an armor of distance, anonymity, and instant disengagement coupled with the threat of unmasking intimate desire. Thus trolling the social space of the dating/hookup app potentially subverts the power structures, economies, and etiquettes—visible and invisible—of material social spaces.

Whether physical or digital, publications, exhibitions, and reviews leave deliberate traces—calculated one-sided arguments that only feed capitalist modes of production. The politics of cyber-sex inherent in Scruff may provide a place outside the very public arena of architectural production, education, and publication to engage in meaningful criticism.

To address the emergence of digital media on and within architecture, critic Sylvia Lavin notably employs the metaphor of the kiss. "Kissing is not a collaboration between two that aims to make one unified thing," she argues. "It is the intimate friction between two mediums that produces twoness—reciprocity without identity—which opens new epistemological and formal models for redefining architecture's relation to other mediums and hence to itself."[10] Is trolling—a metaphor like kissing applied to the built environment via methods of digital communication such as dating and hookup apps—a valid contemporary critical position?

From recent initiatives like Turncoats and the Architectural Association's AAgora, the state of criticism in architecture remains a central concern. Turncoats, a new debate format founded by Phineas Harper and Maria Smith, describes the current trend of architectural panels as "lukewarm love-ins, critically impotent, elitist and stuffy."[11] Yet, they employ sexualized metaphors to articulate their point. According to Turncoats, desire may be the only solution to criticism's impotency.

In Lavin's conception of the kiss, however, friction is paramount. Burdened by the weight of the profession—associations, academic roles and the small, nebulous communities in which architectural culture is produced—meaningful criticism is reduced to two binary poles: "lukewarm love-ins" or grandiose Patrick Schumacher-esque provocations. Otherwise, contemporary criticism is confined to one-sided arguments that play out across digital publishing platforms or drawn-out entries in the comments section. These confrontations are more narcissistic than critical, more akin to kissing your reflection than another individual.

Lavin argues that kissing has the potential to redefine relations between architecture and other mediums, which apps already enable in virtual space and dating/hook apps may further offer. In Andres Jacque's aptly titled film *Pornified Homes*, exhibited at the 2016 Oslo Architecture Triennial, he examines the manner in which online escort services have begun reshaping London's Chelsea neighborhood. In the film, a formless narrator coos, "Colonial creation of a geography of center and periphery might now be replaced by a layered coexistence in which the architecture of properness—the one that accommodates law firms, wealthy residences

9
For example, major exhibitions like "Modern Architecture: International Exhibition" in 1932 to Mark Wigley's 1988 "Deconstructivist Architecture" were important methods to circulate architectural knowledge/criticism in a similar regard as Denise Scott Brown, Robert Venturi and Steven Izenour's *Learning From Las Vegas* in 1972.

10
Sylvia Lavin, *Kissing Architecture* (Princeton: Princeton Architectural Press, 2011), 23.

11
"Turncoats," *Turncoats*, accessed February 17, 2018, http://turncoats. world/.

12
Andres Jacque, *Pornified Homes*
(Oslo: Oslo Architecture Triennial,
2016).

and corporative headquarters—contains a secluded and sexualized backyard architecture of otherness."[12] The act of trolling through dating apps provides a similar potential in virtual space by conflating sexuality, etiquette and criticism—flattening the distance between center and periphery as well as the hierarchies or taxonomies of properness produced through modernist education and professionalism.

Architecture has long been weaponized against queer people to conceal or suppress desire, yet as shown above, desire can be weaponized against these same institutional and capitalist forces. Though instant gratification has been employed by app developers to market sexualized lifestyles to queer male consumers, trolling is a deliberately disobedient strategy: anti-capitalist resistance in virtual space. "What for me is important is to register what are the new forms of accountability, subversion and disobedience that we need to emerge within them," Jacque argues. "The complexity of our societies depends on our capacity to bring alternatives into apps and to render them spaces of queerized contestation."[13] Trolling provides an alternative mode to contest institutional frameworks—the academic model and the social space of the hookup app—by subverting circulations of power and knowledge. It flirts with the role these apps may play in architectural culture beyond capitalist development.

13
Jake Charles Rees, "Andres Jacque,
Sex Apps, and Intimate Strangers
- A Candid Interview," *Run Riot!*,
September 11, 2016.

Recently, I encountered the architect I trolled in person when we shared space on a review panel. While apprehensive at first, we soon joked over the rift between our URL and IRL personas as well as the inevitable awkwardness of meeting in person. Later that day, I looked down at my phone to see another message—this time without a Woof or Eggplant emoji—discussing future projects. It appeared as if my trolling had opened a new space for critical engagement between us, or a more open platform for sharing perspectives that counter the capitalist foundations of architectural education, practice, and criticism. Lavin has called a critical kiss a bite, but perhaps we could also call it a Woof.

Angles of Incidence: Film, Mirrors, and Architectural Plot Twists

Austin Edwards

fig. 1 (facing)
City of Mirrors

1
Fletcher Markel and Alfred
Hitchcock, "CBC Telescope
Interview," *Mr. Biography*, 1964,
www.mrbiography.com/bio/
hitchcock/i-telescope.html.

When the great filmmaker Alfred Hitchcock was asked to explain the concept of montage, he said it was "the assembly of pieces of film that, when moved in rapid succession before the eye, create an idea."[1] Latent in his answer is his own deep knowledge of Russian visionaries Sergei Eisenstein and Lev Kuleshov, who not only recognized the potential power of montage, but realized how it could leverage an audience. Montage was not just a directorial choice but a narrative tool, a composition that could be honed and crafted with extreme intention. Also latent in Hitchock's definition, though he does specify film as his medium, is the idea that montage is not a tool available only to the filmmaker. We must ask, then: can montage in architecture leverage an audience as successfully as film? What are the mechanisms by which this can be accomplished, and to what effect?

The Kuleshov Effect and "Sequential Art"

In order to identify some of the more radical ways montage might be used to affect an audience for architecture, let us look at a powerful example from film. Figure 2a (on the following page) shows a series of still images from Wan Kar Wai's film *In The Mood For Love*, which we can use to reconstruct a series of events: Chow watches two women talk. One leaves, and the other speaks to Chow. Chow ascends a set of stairs, looking at a piece of paper. He enters a hallway and rings a doorbell.

Though we were only able to use stills, the result of viewing the series

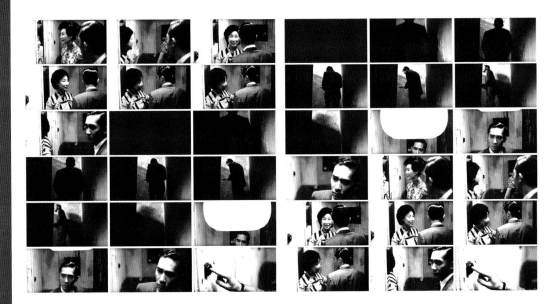

fig. 2a & 2b
Stills from *In the Mood for Love*.

2

Scott McCloud, *Understanding Comics: The Invisible Art* (New York: William Morrow, 1994), 1-70.

of images is sufficient in proving Hitchcock's assertion. In fact, using still images may be an even more pronounced example of how viewers formulate ideas based on sequential elements. In Scott McCloud's acclaimed work *Understanding Comics*, he describes the ability of any series of actions to be divided into "sequential art," wherein a set of actions is divided into panels (in the case of our example, frames) with white space between them.[2] While the pictorial representations themselves show what actions are taking place, the white space (the "gutter") shows the passage of time. We as viewers can inherently understand that when two sequential images show Chow on one stair, then the next stair up, that he is ascending. The margin between the frames and lack of actual motion does not hinder the conception of action or the time-rate of change of that action. In short, the still images form an idea of motion, an idea of things happening in time, and the idea that Chow's exchange with the woman eventually led him to that hallway.

While it is easy to demonstrate the ability of sequential art like comics and film to precipitate ideas, the accuracy of those ideas is worth further investigation. Let us look again at the same set of stills from *In The Mood For Love*, slightly rearranged (fig. 2b). Analyzing in the same way as before, we come up with a new set of actions over time: Chow ascends a set of stairs, looking at a piece of paper. He encounters two women talking. One leaves, and the other speaks to Chow. He rings a doorbell.

We can see the problem already. This series of events seems as logical as the previous series we constructed (fig. 2a) based on what we know, so which is correct? Is one more correct than the other? The answer is no, insofar as they both successfully illustrate a logical series of events—even though the second order (fig. 2b) was the one that actually appeared in Wai's film. The important outcome of this experiment is the realization that in both cases the viewer can look at the images and reconstruct the totality of a set of actions in time, even though you were not given all of the information. Fading to black, for example, is

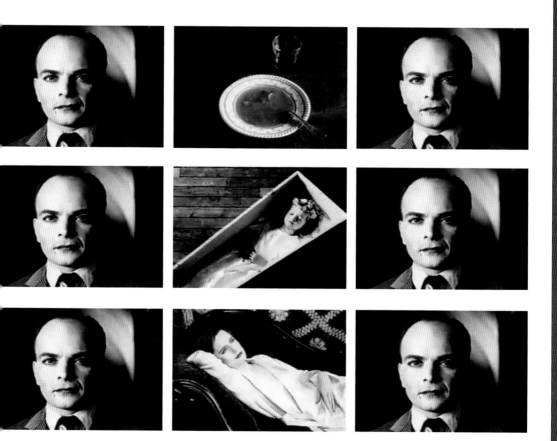

fig. 3
Mousjokine's subtle range of
reactions to varied stimuli.

imbued with temporal meaning: the black scene in the first example is assumed as a linear jump forward in time, when it could have been a step backwards chronologically that the audience was hitherto unaware of. Ultimately, the way in which the scenes were presented—linearly in sequence—caused the audience to imbue even a solid black screen as not only chronologically, geographically, and narratively significant, but significant in a particular temporal, spatial, and narrative direction.

The relationship of presentation to ideation is exactly what Lev Kuleshov noticed when analyzing his audience. In a now-famous experiment, Kuleshov assembled a montage of actor Ivan Mousjokine making a facial expression. Prior to each shot of Mousjokine's face were three other shots: one of a bowl of soup, one of a girl in a casket, and one of a woman lying down (fig. 3). To the audience, Mousjokine was seeing the soup and reacting with dismay, seeing the casket and reacting with sadness, seeing the woman and reacting with lust.[3]

Several sources site that the audience "raved about the acting," and that they were astounded by Mousjokine's "subtlety and range."[4] In each case, however, the actor's face had remained exactly the same. The audience had ascribed an emotion to his expression based on what was shown in the preceding shot, even though the shots were otherwise unrelated. Not only that, but the audience had assumed that the expressions were due to the preceding shot, and not a prescient reaction to the following

3
Eric Fritts, "The Kuleshov Effect:
Understanding Video Editing's Most
Powerful Tool," *Videomaker*, July
21, 2015, https://www.videomaker.
com/article/c10/18236-the-
kuleshov-effect-understanding-
video-editing%E2%80%99s-most-
powerful-tool

4
Caroline O'Donnell, *Niche Tactics:
Generative Relationships Between
Architecture and Site* (London:
Routledge, 2015), 137-153.

shot. Finally, and most amazingly, the audience had assumed that all three expressions were different, even though they were exactly the same. Kuleshov had discovered an astounding way in which his audience was processing the information he presented. This phenomenon, now called "The Kuleshov Effect," illustrates the ability of the audience to derive meaning from sequential shots, freeing the filmmaker from explicitly showing every action a character takes, or remaining bound to a singular increment of time within a story.[5] It proved the viewer's ability to form an assumption about information that isn't explicitly shown. It also proved the filmmaker's ability to use those assumptions to misinform for narrative benefit. We know this benefit by a more common name: the plot twist.

5
Evan Puschak, "Arrival: A Response to Bad Movies," *The Nerdwriter*, accessed 15 Feb. 2017, www.youtube.com/watch?v=z18LY6NME1s.

Montage and Architecture

While Kuleshov contributed to our understanding of the power of montage, his contemporary Sergei Eisenstein was fascinated with the ways in which architecture achieved montage. Citing Auguste Choisy's study of the Acropolis, he discusses the power of experiencing a space as a sequence of cinematic shots and the impression left on the viewer.

As Caroline O'Donnell points out in her book *Niche Tactics*, one may recognize that a similar analysis had been done some 18 years earlier in Le Corbusier's *Vers une architecture*. His examination stressed the idea of what he called "architectural promenade," wherein "architectural spectacle offers itself consecutively to the view." O'Donnell's writing, especially when read alongside Flora Samuel's *Le Corbusier and the Architectural Promenade*, paint a picture of Corbusier's promenade as "an architecture of initiation." This refers to the idea that architecture could only be understood by moving through it in its entirety; the unfolding of each particular space was a result of the viewer's active engagement with every point along the line of circulation, each of them "offering aspects constantly varied, unexpected, and sometimes astonishing." Samuel goes on to say that the intended effect of this is to "resensitise [*sic*] people to their surroundings." In less explicit terms, Corbusier posits that architectural elements and their arrangement "speak to" the viewer.[6]

6
Flora Samuel, "Introduction," in *Le Corbusier and the Architectural Promenade*, (Basel: Birkhauser, 2010), 9-23.

There is something in this quote that Eisenstein's analysis lacks. The way in which Corbusier's explanation highlights the ability of montage to surprise but also to orient is much more homologous with Kuleshov's description of audience orientation. What we are now faced with are Corbusien ideas aligning with those of Kuleshov and Hitchcock. Namely, architectural sequence and arrangement suggests an orientation—a spatial idea. If an assumption about space can be precipitated by architecture, can it be subverted? Can architects find a mechanism to suggest an architectural Kuleshov Effect? Is there such a thing as an architectural plot twist?

Hong Kong as Film and City

Examining the Acropolis through Choisy's diagrammatic explanations or Corbusier's rhetoric, it is hard to conceive of architectural space that isn't

fig. 4
Mirrored facades in Hong Kong

7

Richard Koeck, "The Tectonics of Film Space" in *Film, Mind and Body* (London: Routledge, 2013), 31-38.

8

mise en abyme - literally translated as "placed into abyss" refers to a frame within a frame, or the occurrence of an image within itself

highly designed being able to elicit montage. But one has only to step into any environment, especially a city, to see that the same attributes described by Eisenstein—shot design, shot depth, shot length, visual multidimensionality—are all present. In fact, both Jean Baudrillard and David B. Clarke have asserted that in order to truly understand a city, one should look to its representation on film before analyzing it directly. This is something that Clarke refers to as the "conceptualization of cityscape as screenscape," where the tectonics of the city become a hybrid of their actual spatial configuration and their cinematographic representation.[7] By definition, this approach requires both a first-person and a cinematic experience of the city. However, the argument can be made that certain cities challenge the separation of those experiences. In particular, Hong Kong seems to blur the line between a city understood on screen and a city understood as screens—a city that is itself *mise-en-abyme*.[8] This is partially due to its sheer physical and sensory density, but is mainly the result of the extreme proliferation of mirrored surfaces at all scales.

Mirror has curious implications for the creation of cinematic space. It has the ability to suggest space where it does not exist, but also cannot do so without showing space that does. It is limited in its capacity by interactions with light and geometry. It is at once three-dimensional and two-dimensional, heterotopic and utopic, a superimposition of reality and projection. The irony, and potentially the genius here, is that all of these things could also be said of celluloid film. This is to say that Hong Kong's literal *mise-en-abyme* (the experience of the reflected city being an undifferentiable part of the experience of the actual city) makes Hong Kong simultaneously filmic and real. While currently the mirrored surfaces that make this condition possible go largely unnoticed, they are the mechanism by which architectural plot twists can be intentionally achieved.

Angles of Incidence

Angles of Incidence, an architectural proposal for the Hong Kong Central Film Archive, is an attempt to realize the actual forms that these plot twists take, and to understand their relationships to program, spatial organization, scale, and context. Through rigorous experimentation, observation, film study, and design documentation, three particular strategies—and three specific scales—emerged within the design and its relationship to an existing building on the site.

The first of these strategies takes place on the scale of the entire building and heavily leverages the existing building for effect; therefore, it is important that the existing condition be thoroughly explained. The site of the proposal is a derelict Bauhaus market building in the Central District of Hong Kong, originally built in 1938 and abandoned since 2003. Though the market itself is closed, the northwestern part of the third floor operates as part of Hong Kong's extensive raised pedestrian network, including a southwestern connection to the "people mover," the world's longest escalator. Before any other considerations were made, the intervention had to first tackle these existing conditions, the building's historic status, and its potential for use, renovation, and augmentation. This consideration became the first opportunity to subvert expectation, and led to what could be referred to as "*mise-en-abyme* as preservation"—a twist on the rampant instances of whole-building reflections seen throughout the city.

To accomplish this, the building, which is symmetrical across its long and short axes, was cut in half along the short axis. The southwest half of the existing building was preserved, and the northeast half was demolished so an addition to the building could be designed. The important element in this strategy was to place a large, mirrored glass curtain wall along the centerline of the cut, which mirrored the existing building and hid the addition from view. The result is reflection which recreates the totality of the original building, causing it to look as though it has not been changed at all. This is particularly effective since the mirrored wall faces the people mover, which allows an elevated viewing platform upon approach. In addition, the direction the wall faces takes advantage of the relatively low height of the market, using the remaining portion as a spacer to allow lines of sight from higher buildings to the south.

The mirage of total symmetry, and the expectation it sets up, is further complemented by the complete reversal of positive and negative space on the north side of the wall, subverting the spatial expectation suggested by the reflection we could see as we walked toward the building. The idea here is twofold: this example of *mise-en-abyme* acts as a sort of spatial archive, recalling the previous configuration of the building and nodding to the film archival program of its successor It also calls attention to the bizarre nature of buildings clad in reflective surfaces. By tricking the eye with one building façade, viewers start to notice the instances of this effect that already exist in the building's vicinity—the trick is not just the one-off surprise within the proposed building, but an experience that

fig. 5 (previous spread)
The design allows neighboring mirrors to penetrate inside.

fig. 6 (facing)
Museum rooms can be experienced through mere projection of space.

causes viewers to question their expectations within the city.

While several choices about the addition were in service to the first of these twists—namely which way the curtain wall should face and how tall the new building should be—they were decisions that could not be made without also considering twist (and scale) number two: the use of existing mirrored façades to accomplish impossible lines of sight. The most apparent example of this is the use of the existing Hang Seng Bank building, which crowds the site on its northeast side with teal-colored, highly reflective glass panels. By keeping the northeast façade of the addition all varying opacities of glass, large active spaces like projection galleries can be viewed from other floors, other buildings, and even around the corner on the street level, while more private programs like sound stages and classrooms can remain opaque but mirrored, participating in the dance of sightlines.

The lines of sight set up expectations about what may lie below, above, or next to the space a viewer currently inhabits, but the same surface that allows us to see that next space also differentiates its experience once we are inside. Relationships to other, oblique façades, the façade previously used, or programmatic relationships between previously unseen spaces do much to subvert the suggestion first formed by the more omniscient view. The intention here is to once again call attention to the context and rely on the existing cinematic hybridity of Hong Kong. The mirrored façades participate in the program of the building, acting as screens onto which the activity, program, exhibitions, and content are projected and showcased to the city and the person. Maybe to the chagrin of the docents and curators, the museums and galleries can be visited in part just by movement through the area around the archive: a montage of first-, second-, and third-hand projections.

The final strategy is seen in part at this contextual scale, but may be more accurately and effectively described at the smaller scale, where building elements like fascia, handrails, polished floors, windows, and metallic columns create visual confusion. In almost all of these cases, spatial information is condensed into a panelized sequence much like McCloud's

fig. 7 (facing and above)
Moving through sequences of
human-scaled spaces can create
scenarios of architectural plot twists.

comic art. The result is the presentation of non-geographically linear spaces as visually linear. The experience of these types of spatial, reflective thresholds causes a moment of orientation, severe spatial discrepancy, and subsequent reorientation. In more filmic terms, the mirror presents a montage from which information is derived and then completely jumbled and upended, only to be redressed by an epiphanous understanding of both the mechanism and the actual sequence.

This effect, while radically different in scale than the first two, may be both the most present in Hong Kong and the most literally cinematic, mirroring closely the "aha moment" the audience experiences during a film's major plot revelation. Additionally, it informs the majority of the actual space within the addition, where the sloped geometry of theaters allows for periscopic effects; the use of mirrors, projectors, and windows allow for moments of overlap and interference; and these discordant smaller elements allow for dialogue with larger scales already discussed.

It seems demonstrable through this proposal that mirrors possess the ability to subvert and enhance the narrative power of montage, or promenade, on several scales. Reflection, it seems, levels the field between the architect, the director, and the screenwriter, allowing architecture to achieve the fullness of Kuleshovian control—a tool for misinformation and re-information—which helps the audience to achieve a "varied, unexpected, and sometimes astonishing" experience of which both Corbusier and Hitchcock would approve. 🐰

The Mischief of Venice

Phoebe Crisman and Michael Petrus

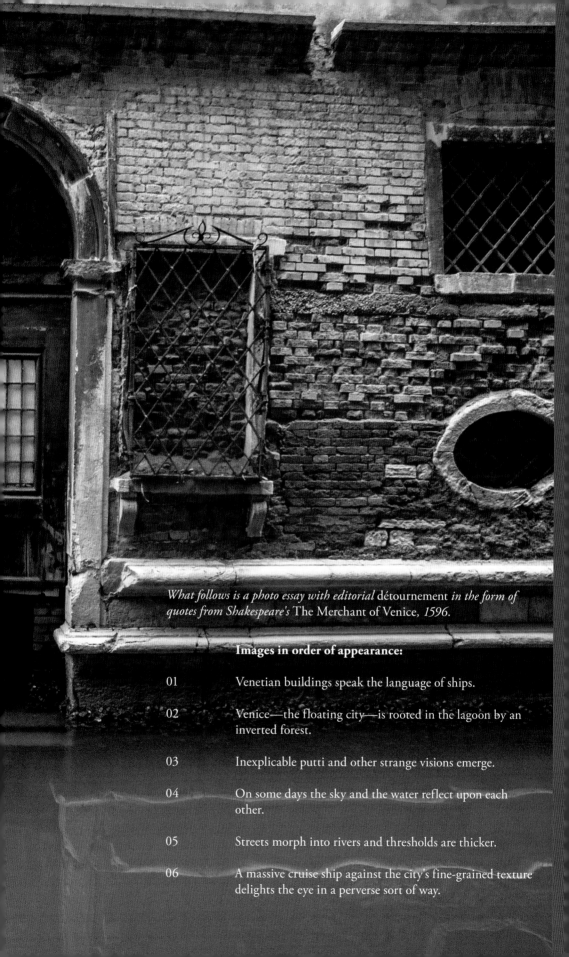

What follows is a photo essay with editorial détournement *in the form of quotes from Shakespeare's* The Merchant of Venice, *1596.*

Images in order of appearance:

01   Venetian buildings speak the language of ships.

02   Venice—the floating city—is rooted in the lagoon by an inverted forest.

03   Inexplicable putti and other strange visions emerge.

04   On some days the sky and the water reflect upon each other.

05   Streets morph into rivers and thresholds are thicker.

06   A massive cruise ship against the city's fine-grained texture delights the eye in a perverse sort of way.

ANTONIO
In sooth, I know not why I am so sad:
It wearies me; you say it wearies you;
But how I caught it, found it, or came by it,
What stuff 'tis made of, whereof it is born,
I am to learn;
And such a want-wit sadness makes of me,
That I have much ado to know myself.

GRATIANO
Let me play the fool:
With mirth and laughter let old wrinkles come,
And let my liver rather heat with wine
Than my heart cool with mortifying groans.
Why should a man, whose blood is warm within,
Sit like his grandsire cut in alabaster?
Sleep when he wakes and creep into the jaundice
By being peevish?

LORENZO
O dear discretion, how his words are suited!
The fool hath planted in his memory
An army of good words; and I do know
A many fools, that stand in better place,
Garnish'd like him, that for a tricksy word
Defy the matter.

GRATIANO

That ever holds: who riseth from a feast
With that keen appetite that he sits down?
Where is the horse that doth untread again
His tedious measures with the unbated fire
That he did pace them first? All things that are,
Are with more spirit chased than enjoy'd.

PORTIA
That light we see is burning in my hall.
How far that little candle throws his beams!
So shines a good deed in a naughty world.

The State of Things is Very Serious.

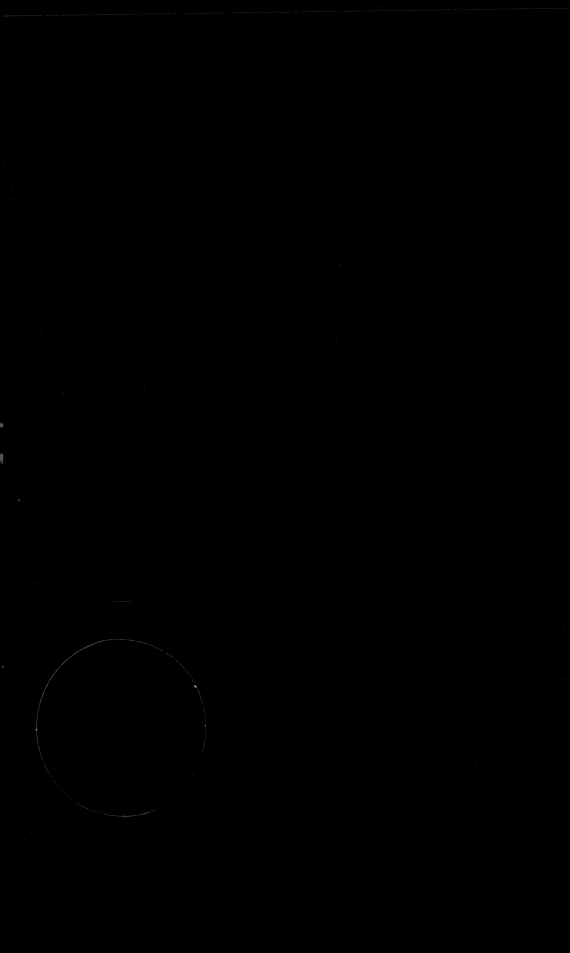

From Edward Morris Opler, "Coyote Comes to Life Four Times," in *Myths and Tales of the Jicarilla Apache Indians* (Mineola, NY: Dover Publications, 1994).

"Coyote had a plan which he knew he could carry out by means of his power. He took his heart out and cut it in half. He put one half right at the tip of his nose and the other half at the end of his tail."

"Explore Everything": A Conversation with Bradley Garrett

The Editors

fig. 1 (facing)
An abandoned Napoleonic era
coastal defense sea fort that can
only be accessed at low tide. Garrett
trapped himself there for three days
and camped out.
(Photo: Bradley Garrett)

1
Bradley Garrett, *Explore Everything:
Place-hacking the City* (London:
Verso, 2014).

Colin (L): Your book *Explore Everything*,[1] and much of your work, involves unlocking closed-off urban spaces. Why do you think that it's important to investigate spaces that we don't typically have access to?

Bradley (B): It's a very geographic question; it's a question about space, and questions of space are always wrapped up in questions of power. Who built what is around us? What do we have access to? Why do we have access to those spaces? So many people go through life without ever questioning where they are or why they have access to some places and not others. I feel that it doesn't take very much to develop a critical edge that begins to push you into this whole other realm of understanding.

I used to be an archaeologist, so I dealt with time more than space, but there is a similar awareness cultivated when you're working on an excavation and suddenly start pulling out these varied layers of history. It fundamentally changes how you imagine the dimensions of the space you're in. The kind of exploration that I've been doing—mostly trespassing—and that I'm trying to encourage people to engage with prompts similar questions. When you start crossing over boundaries, particularly when you have confrontations with other people about whether you have the right to be in those places, then suddenly that apparatus of power which is normally hidden becomes apparent and that enables us to have a critical dialogue. A lot of those boundaries are invisible and once they spring up then we can probe and question them. All of the exploration that I've been undertaking is about trying to cultivate that critical sensibility.

L: How have people typically reacted when they've found you on their property? Are you usually able to get your message across and engage in this sort of dialogue that you're talking about or does the whole thing turn into a run from the cops?

B: Interestingly, most people are just fascinated or confused. You'll run into a security guard for instance—someone paid to look after this site who is used to pacing around in boredom as nothing tends to happen while they're on the clock. Then suddenly this event unfolds in front of them: there's someone coming over the fence and their immediate reaction I'm sure is to think there's something nefarious going on, that these are thieves or people coming to damage the property. Then we chat with the guards and tell them that we're just interested and want to take photos. Sometimes they'll actually take us around and say we don't need to hop the fence and can just knock at the front gate.

There's a kind of liberation that comes from silencing the cop in your head and getting back to the state we were in when we were kids.

So you have to gauge whether it makes more sense to ask permission or to ask forgiveness after you're caught. Every situation is different—if you go to a construction site then they're going to have all sorts of concerns about insurance liability and there's no way they're going to let you on the site. Or if you're sneaking into parts of public infrastructure, especially transportation infrastructure, for obvious reasons people get nervous about that. I find that in those situations, once someone has already decided that this is not something that's ever going to be allowed under any circumstances, you can't really reason with them. It's hard to initiate a conversation where you can explain your motivations and intentions and turn someone on to your perspective. But those situations are few and far between I find, and actually if you explain to people why you're doing what you're doing they will usually get it.

Most people share that innate curiosity, it's just that we suppress it in ourselves. This is the cop in our head that constantly prevents us from saying things, doing things, going to certain places. Everyone understands that there's a kind of liberation that comes from silencing the cop in your head and getting back to the state we were in when we were kids. You run around and try things out and you don't worry about it until it goes wrong.

L: In some ways your work reminds me of the Situationist International and their concept of the *dérive*—finding your way through a city based on intuition and experiencing it as a random sequence of spaces. Is this how you engage with urban space? Not necessarily random, but more ignoring or passing beyond the prescribed boundaries within built environments. I was wondering if you have advice for the average person who is trying to experience

fig. 2
Causeway to get to the sea fort from
the English coast
(Photo: Bradley Garrett)

this kind of interaction with the city and engage with spaces that they normally don't.

B: Well I think the Situationists were much less intentional with what they were doing. When we're going out to explore a location, particularly in the context of urban exploration, there's usually a specific location we want to go to. We scope out the security patrols and we try to understand how that site functions before we tackle it. It's not very often that urban exploration emerges from a spontaneous drift. It's a different kind of urban exploration I think, different from a drift toward emerging affects where you just kind of let the city take you places. I could imagine that the Situationist perspective on urban exploration would be that this is actually a kind of anti-*dérive*, that there's no chance about it—this is a very specific moment of penetration through the veil. We are very forcefully manufacturing situations.

But I do think that there is a politics to both of those things. I think about Walter Benjamin with his beautiful notion of "brushing history against the grain" and feel like the Situationists brush space against the grain because the flow of the city is primarily constructed by capitalist forces. Everywhere we go is dictated by where we live, where we're shopping and where we're working. We're going to the café, we're going to work, we're going to the grocery store, and it's not very often that we find ourselves moving through space in a way that is not dictated by consumer behavior.

fig. 3
A sixteenth-century fortification on
the island Malta
(Photo: Bradley Garrett)

I think that's the beauty of what the Situationists are doing, for instance, in laying an algorithm over the city and moving through the city in random patterns—it disrupts that notion that everything needs to flow according a particular social narrative. We forget everything around us is a social construct. There's absolutely no reason why we need to move in the way we do or go to the places we go except that things have been constructed to encourage or even coerce us into moving in that way. So, moving a different way is always a political act, whether that's totally intentional or a spontaneous drift.

To answer your question then, I think that people should do what inspires them. And anything that gets you to move in a different way, experience different places—that's an opportunity. Whether that requires taking a field guide out with you or being very pointed in your explorations, or whether it's just about walking out the door and letting go of any sense of destination or goals—these are all positive disruptions. It does not even have to require much effort; even just walking home from work, we think we've found the most efficient route and we'll just keep walking it over and over again. All you have to do sometimes is just kind of drift over one street and suddenly you start discovering all this other stuff.

I think that part of it is about exposing yourself to these spaces, but I also think there's a kind of sensibility to be cultivated where you're open

fig. 4
During a field trip with Will Self's psychogeography class at Brunel, University of London, Garrett snuck into a trash dump.
(Photo: Bradley Garrett)

to space. You're paying attention to people's interactions, you're trying to seek out the liminal, the weird, the funky, and if you let those things come to you then they will. I'm always struck by how much fortuitous spontaneity is suppressed by everyday life; just the kinds of structures and rhythms that we become accustomed to. When you have these surreal moments where you see something happen and you don't look away but rather just stay with it and hold on to it, something unfolds in a way that is reminiscent of childhood, where life was dictated by impulsiveness and encounters and that search for the interesting and the novel. Those are differences that makes everyday life memorable. I always feel like if I have a day where I haven't explored everything, where I've just gone through the structures and routines that either I've imposed on myself or someone has imposed on me, then I just end up laying there in bed at night depressed, thinking "what was the point of this day?" At that point I might just get up and put on fishing waders and go trudge through a sewer because what have you got to lose?

L: As architects and designers, we often try to force public space into our projects—I think this is an innate desire for a lot of architects. And then ultimately this public space will tend to get reduced and become private or will just end up not getting used and become an ineffective space. I'm wondering as somebody who's explored a lot of different kinds of spaces, many of which have fallen out of use, how you think we might be able to make more effective public space, and

also how we can preserve public spaces in cities that are constantly getting denser and more expensive to live in.

B: Well I think the linchpin here is that we have to abandon the notion of planning. Even if space is created for people, say for a public space, sanctioned graffiti zone or a skate park, the act of giving it over is also an act of holding onto power. It's those in power saying, "I am going to grant you the ability to have access to this space," when what people gain the most agency from is the process of colonizing something and letting the *ad hoc* become settled over time and through use. If there's any kind of organic community formation that starts to move into those interstitial spaces that we can't quite figure out what to do with, I feel like we should encourage that. The problem is how do we facilitate that without taking control of it?

We can get there, but it's a big ask. Let's be honest, it would require abandoning the entire premise of architecture under the neoliberal order that values economic production over social value. As it is, everything needs to be economically viable, and we've got to comply with insurance and liability and all that. So how do we let that go and how do we instead prioritize the kind of organic emergence of the social? How do we encourage that to happen without dictating that it happens? That, I feel, is the kind of linchpin in this. It's what fails to happen in a lot of development projects.

But you see it in a lot of other places. Interestingly, these are often places where they don't have the resources to do social policing. I was in Phnom Penh in Cambodia a couple of years ago and visited this derelict Olympic stadium. Local communities started colonizing it: first clearing out the running track and running on it, but then having informal aerobics classes, and then vendors moved in and started barbecuing corn and now suddenly there's this whole hive of activity. All of it was unpermitted and unsanctioned, but it was gorgeous—it was all just happening. These were the things that people wanted in their community and they just colonized the space to make it work. And because the government didn't have the resources to stop it from happening it just kept happening. I feel like there's a lesson to learn there. The dictates under which we all try to work seem to make it impossible to explain to people that this is important. And that if they try to fabricate that same thing, it falls flat.

L: You've been to a lot of different kinds of places. Could you describe the weirdest or most interesting place you've been?

B: There's such a long list of weird places. I did a guest lecture for Will Self; he teaches a class on psychogeography at Brunel in London. I was talking about similar things: the importance of being in the world and making things happen. Suddenly Will turns to me and says, "Then why the hell are we all sitting here? Why are we in this room in this institution having a conversation about the thing we should be doing? Let's go!" So we all left. We walked out of the class and down the river, and suddenly there was a fence on our left. One of the students said, "I think we should hop the fence." So we did, seventeen or eighteen of us, having no idea what was on the other side.

Inside, we climb a hill and come over the other side of it, and it turns out to be a recycling center, a dump. There were these vast piles of metal and plastic; there's this typology of waste that you can see over an entire landscape. We all climbed down in it and started digging through the trash and found all sorts of incredible things like creepy dolls, discarded books, and porn magazines all stuck together in the mold and mildew of the dump. We spent ages digging through this thing and people were finding artifacts and putting them in their bags, when of course the inevitable happens. This guy comes out and he's got a dog, and a trash dump is not a place you want to be caught in. This is the kind of place where they sic the dog on you. I've got this photo of Will Self running over a trash pile, coat blowing in the wind, toward this guy telling him, "Wait, wait, hold on! This is psychogeography!" And by the end, the guy had no idea what we were doing. He was completely confused, and kind of just like, "Whatever, you guys seem to be really into this trash." It worked out, but I have to say it was one of the stranger experiences I've had in my life and it did emerge from a spontaneous exploration, which I like. There was no plan there, it just happened. 🐾

fig. 6 (facing)
Child bathing in a bucket in Phnom Penh, Cambodia.
(Photo: Bradley Garrett)

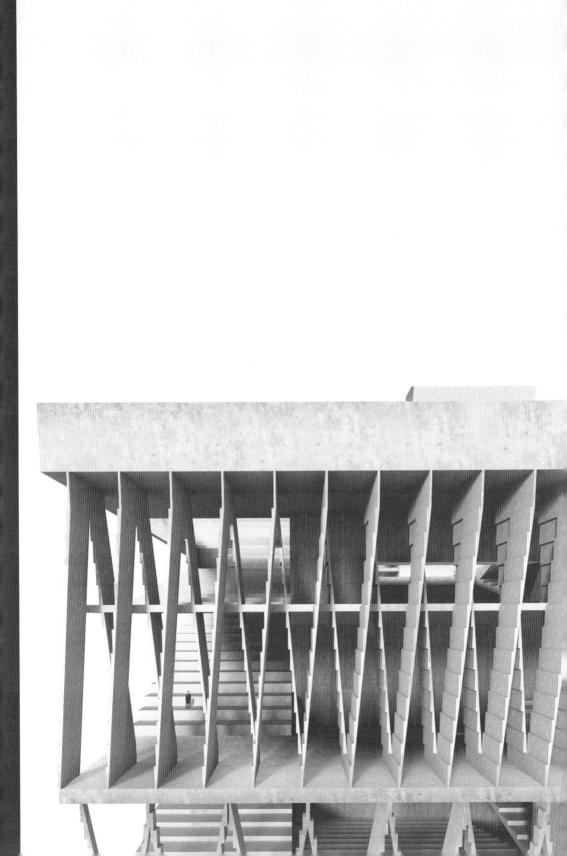

Ad Absurdum

Naomi Maki

I.

Absurdism is the irreconcilable conflict that arises between the tendency to seek meaning and the inability to find any.

It describes the paradoxical condition, where "[the] appetite for the absolute and for unity" meets "the impossibility of reducing this world to a rational and reasonable principle."[1]

1
Albert Camus, *The Myth of Sisyphus* (London: Penguin, 2013).

II.

The act of defining the absurd engages a protocol, a set of instruments and conventions.

In a spatial scenario, we comprehend by establishing a point of reference, a line of reference, a datum. Datum is an act of perception, something that we use as a foundation, from which to construct a sense of understanding as we sequence through space and time.

While concurrently engaging the protocols of scale and datum, absurdity systematically defamiliarizes itself from this.

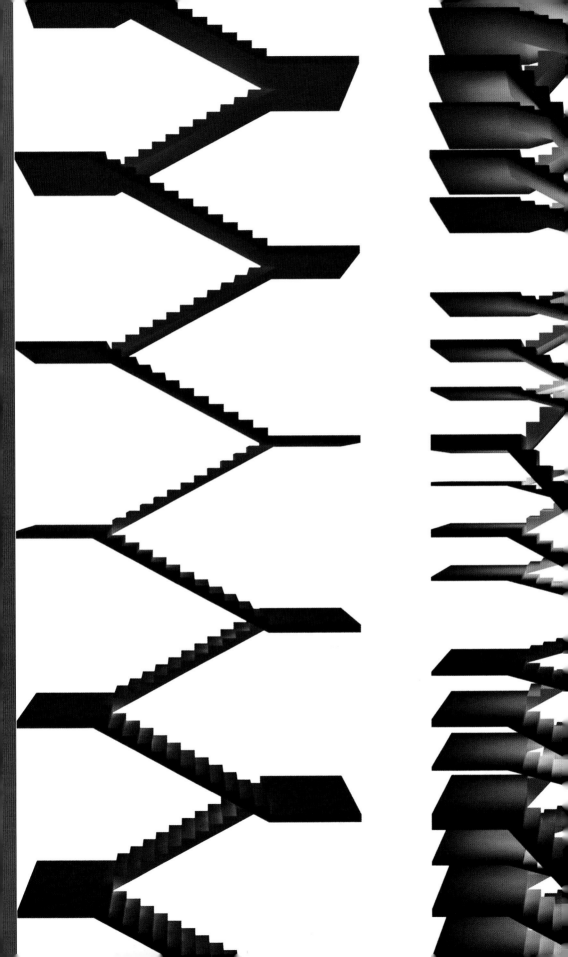

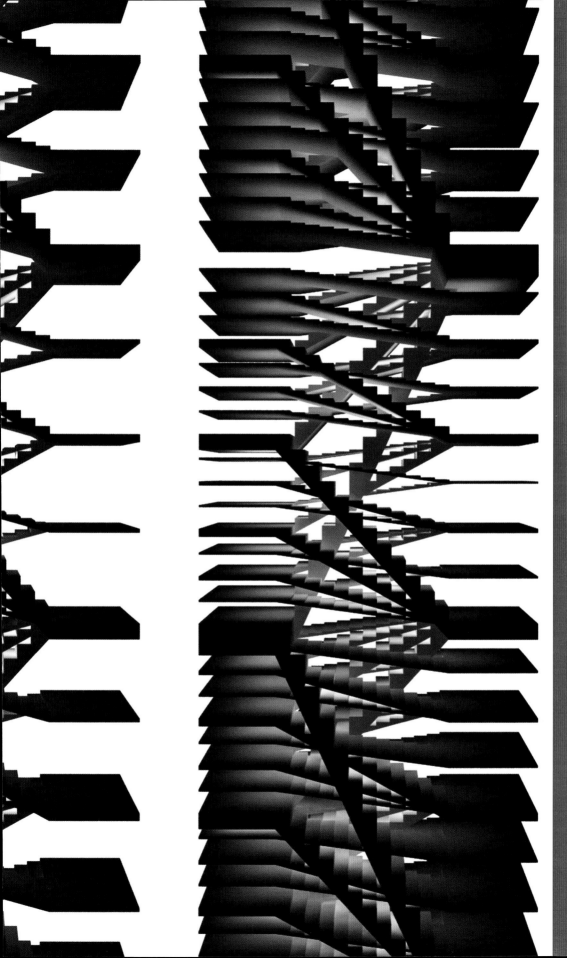

III.

Indifference to convention and value liberates forms to operatively pursue their emergent potentials.

Forms establish autonomous methodologies driven by the evolving syntax of their internal properties.

Expanding upon their basic, internal essences, the unconventional implementation of convention separates form and meaning.

IV.

Scale is an instrument of absurdity.

Its transformative capacities are compounded to produce an array of amalgamated absurdities.

The proliferation of multiple scales, multiple directions, and multiple orientations allows for the systematic speculation of one form's possible architectural manifestations.

Falling down the stairs. Discriminatory hiring practices. Bed bugs. Breaking a bone. Cancer. Incompetence. Incontinence. Hurricanes. North Korea. Diarrhea. Melting ice caps. Identity theft. Anxiety disorders. Abortion. The opioid epidemic. Murder. Cyberbullying. A plague of locusts. AIDS. Asphyxiation. The death of a family pet. Monopolies. Oligopolies. STDs. Train derailments. Neocolonialism. National security. Mudslides. Chlorofluorocarbons. The stomach flu. Drone drug offenses. Emergency water landings. Panic attacks. The Great Depression. Botulism. Cultural appropriation. Home invasion. Breaking a glass. Maxing out your credit card. Microplastics. Meaninglessness. Kidnapping. Being Domestic violence. The Israeli-Palestinian conflict. Funerals. Waking a sleeping dragon. Self-hatred. Getting fired. War. Scabies. Tsunamis. Overcrowding. A faulty parachute. Meteor collision. Mass extinction. Stock market crash. Poverty. reef bleaching. Invasive species. Hospital bombings. Alcoholism. Anaphylaxis. Leprosy. Tornadoes. Wildfires. Torture. Fault. GMOs. Testicular torsion. Chronic loneliness. Crumbling infrastructure. Riots. Bubonic plague. Bad sex. an elevator. Getting mugged. A loveless marriage. Stepping on a sea urchin. The slow heat death of the universe. Erectile Volcano eruptions. Subprime mortgage lending. Bisphenol-A. Romantic nationalism. Rape culture. Heavy traffic. Shitty intrusion. Postmodern malaise. Air pollution. Ocean acidification. Xenophobia. Acid mine drainage. Poor management. in your bed into a monstrous vermin. Childhood asthma. Bomb cyclones. Gentrification. Breech delivery. Internalized defects. Greenwashing. Sexual assault. Life in prison. Being hit by a car. Being hit by a bus. Being hit by a train. Accidental Unemployment. Sea level rise. Noisy neighbors. When the spectacle is capital to such a degree of accumulation that The plutocracy. State surveillance. Night terrors. Cardiac arrest. Animal abuse. Software vulnerabilities. Corporate tax subsidence. Human suffering. Tooth decay. Major surgery. Bridge collapse. A prison break. Social exile. Phytoplankton crises. Homelessness. Yellow journalism. Deforestation. Malware. Fear of missing out. Losing your keys. Hydrogenated phone in the toilet. Unrequited love. Getting lost. Intimacy issues. Losing your life savings in a Ponzi scheme. A boating he ice. Internet addiction. School shootings. Killing your father and marrying your mother. Cutting the wrong wire. Collusion. Nihilism. Being put on hold. Getting left on read. Lone wolves. Commodity fetishism. Boko Haram. E-waste. ines. Global catastrophic risks. Soggy cereal. Factory farming. Defunded public radio. Printer jams. Stray bullets.

The Trump administration. The military-industrial complex. Gun culture. Forgetting your wallet. Failing a midterm. Shark attacks. Vaccine shortages. Earthquakes. Modern love. Aging. Building collapse. The obesity epidemic. Terrorism. Smog. Accidentally sitting on a cactus. Groundwater contamination. Going through puberty. Divorce. Diabetes. Blunt trauma. Overfishing. Slave labor. Sewage. Termite infestations. Getting struck by lightning. Global warming. warfare. Flash floods. A flat tire. Academic jargon. Asbestos. Self-harm. Mountaintop removal. Sepsis. Ennui. Minor Hemophilia. Human trafficking. Sleep paralysis. Wardrobe malfunction. Alienation of the worker from their product. orphaned. Being stalked. Hearing loss. A terrible haircut. Amputation. Scandal. Libel. The Great Pacific Garbage Patch. Storm surge. Bureaucratic waste. Bad parents. Mistranslation. Getting deported. Falling into a wood chipper. Rabies. Domestic terrorism. Spider bites. Infertility. Urban renewal. Breaking a priceless antique. ISIS. Night blindness. Coral Falling off a cliff. Gross negligence. Monocultures. Sudden Infant Death Syndrome. Consumerism. The San Andreas Superstorms. Being held hostage. Desertification. Nazism. Avalanches. Trade deficits. Losing a lawsuit. Getting stuck in dysfunction. Student debt. Power outages. Disaster capitalism. Drowning. Carbon monoxide poisoning. Smallpox. wifi. Suicide. Post-industrial ruins. Genocide. Foreign policy. Schizophrenia. Hypothermia. Body shaming. Saltwater Dehydration. Missing your flight. Mass incarceration. 9/11. Crapping your pants. Waking to find yourself transformed oppression. Public humiliation. Illegal dumping. Arachnophobia. Agoraphobia. Being stranded at sea. Stage fright. Birth pregnancy. Over-application of herbicides. Famine. Clinical depression. Predatory lending practices. One-percenters. it becomes an image. Cyberattacks. Getting stabbed. Racism. Crooked cops. Organized crime. Compound interest. loopholes. Money in politics. White privilege. Male privilege. Internal bleeding. Hard drive failure. Being audited. Land die-off. Rampant inflation. Stagnant wages. The shrinking middle class. The tech bubble. Russian hackers. Refugee oils. High treason. Taking a chainsaw to the groin. Becoming entangled in barbed wire. Heartbreak. Dropping your accident. Getting into some quicksand. Not getting any "likes." Slipping into a pit of snakes. Heatstroke. Falling through Pushing the wrong button. Kidney stones. Beached whales. Stampedes. Planned obsolescence. E. coli in your lettuce. Religious extremism. Nuclear security. Gingivitis. Gerrymandering. Drought. Concussions. Ever-increasing rent. Long

V.

This technique of the absurd instigates a process of meaninglessness, selectively putting aside conventions and associations such as function, program, structure, and so on.

As a potentially infinite set, these quasi-architectures evolve to form an archive—a constellation of singularities, composing and unfolding totality. 🐰

"Is That Allowed?": A Conversation with Andrew Holder

The Editors

Colin (L): Your work ranges from architectural studies all the way to abstract exhibitions with a lot between. I've seen it described as "disciplinary architecture" in the way that it values systems of the building rather than specific parts, so I was wondering why you think it is important to subvert this tendency to make individual components like structure apparent in an architectural design.

Andrew (A): You're right—the work spans a range, in part just because of the way we've decided to practice. We spent ten years in practice before I got back into the academy, so there's this big pile of built stuff we weren't really worried about theorizing in academic terms. Then getting back into the academy—it was exactly the opposite, where all of the pressure is on positioning and none of the pressure is on selling to a client or making the thing real. My work of the last couple of years has been trying to bring together the most mundane service-based work with the most abstract academic work. How do we bring these as close together as possible and eventually start to make them the same? I think what you're seeing is essentially starting at one end and leaping to the other with no transition, and then slowly working both ends back toward some sort of a middle.

In terms of the disciplinary moniker, I think it's coming from an interview where the interviewer was reacting to the way I described our recent projects. I usually tell a little story about the history or theory of architecture and then I'll say we identified this one little thing in history that we decided to work on. He called that a "disciplinary" approach because it's constantly looking back toward the history of how architecture has conceived of itself as a way of finding new ways to operate. The label is funny to me simply because all we're doing is looking for little opportunities that we can exploit to make a project. It doesn't so much matter whether those are in history or whether those are out in the world with an actual client; we're always looking for the same little nook that we can exploit. Sometimes we find the same kinds of opportunities within the most mundane building projects.

L: Many of your projects seem to hide structure through creative uses of material or an unusual marriage of material and form. Is your intention to highlight other features or systems within the project instead of elements that make the building function?

A: That's an interesting question because we kind of do the opposite. We don't think about buildings as though they're made of systems. We never analyze a built project by looking first at its structure, then its envelope, then its environmental systems. Instead we look at a building as a collection of discrete objects that have been pressed together densely enough that you can get inside. When you think about buildings that way, the objects you encounter in them always belong to multiple systems. Yes, columns are doing the work of structure in a building, but frequently they're also wrapped in a sort of jacketing or firring that allows you to drop a mechanical chase through or stick a sign on one. For us, objects are a much more interesting consolidation of all of these pressures than thinking about the abstract ability to pull apart systems that never really exist in a purely systemic state after construction is complete. We analyze buildings that interest us from this, let's say, "backward" point of view, but it's also how we think about our own work.

Take, for instance, the project "The Kid Gets Out of the Picture." We did a couple of versions of it but I'm thinking of the one in the Harvard library. The plan for that started with a written list of objects. We knew that there was going to be a galvanized steel pipe three feet in diameter, there were going to be four-by-four posts, there were going to be concrete blocks, and then the design was about how to arrange those things so that they touch each other to make an environment. Structure as a way of reading the project comes up at the moments of physical contact between one thing and another. The way, for instance, that some of the four-by-four posts appear to motivate the deformations of the plaster blanket, so that it looks like a post is lifting up a corner to make a friction fit at that single point of contact between blanket and post. We're much more interested in the rhetoric there at that singular episode than we are in the total system of structure. We would ask, is that a real set of forces at play between post and blanket, or is it entirely pictorial? Is the blanket truly plastic and deformable, or is it instead this inert and rigid piece of concrete? It's about closely thinking through object-to-object connections rather than

Is the blanket truly plastic and deformable, or is it instead this inert and rigid piece of concrete?

fig. 2
"The Kid Gets Out of the Picture"
at the Harvard Graduate School of
Design
(Photo: TheLosAngelesDesignGroup)

thinking of structure as a grid that passes through everything equally.

L: For this project you're talking about, "The Kid Gets Out of the Picture," does this approach to inanimate objects help you understand a historical precedent like the English Picturesque? Or does the precedent inform the material?

A: It's kind of the other way around for us: how did the English Picturesque help us with our problem? It's a case where we're trying to be very savvy opportunists about history and trying to look at places in history where people have been thinking about things that also interest us. When we see something useful, we rush back to that moment in time and try to see how other architects have dealt with the ideas we're thinking about.

On this occasion of returning to the Picturesque, we were thinking about building heterogeneous collections of objects, and we were trying to ask ourselves how diverse this collection of parts could get while still retaining a clear coherence. We just wanted to ask an open question: if you're going to make a list of all the ingredients of an architectural assembly, what all could you throw in there and still maintain a sense of the whole? Could I put a blanket in it? How about a pipe that belongs in more industrial or agricultural applications? Could these things somehow be absorbed to the point of complete naturalization, so they seem

fig. 3
"The Kid Gets Out of the Picture" in
Los Angeles
(Photo: TheLosAngelesDesignGroup)

effortless? The Picturesque can help with questions like these, because the primary protagonists of that period in design were thinking through exactly the same problems.

There was this guy William Gilpin, and as he was travelling around and writing books on forest scenery, he used the term "clump" to describe an object that has formed as a compound of separate entities. First he uses "clump" when he's talking about two trees growing so close together they read like one. Then he goes on and that assembly gets more and more diverse in its constituent parts. He looks at one "clump" that's two living trees and one tree that's been struck by lightning and burned down, but they're all so close together that they read as one object. Then he looks at mosses and lichen that have worked their way in there, and then rocks, and then whole landforms. He has an incredibly elastic imagination about how diverse the constituent parts of an assembly can get but still retain a "natural" unity—or let's say a "conventional" unity. He had no problem sketching up these things to look like one big object even though they're made out of madly dissimilar components.

L: Is there any intentional humor in your work? I get a sense of tricky, playful forms when I look at some of your work, so I'm wondering if that's an intentional part of your design approach or just an unexpected outcome.

A: Humor and tricks are maybe working at two levels. The first way to

YOU ALREADY KNOW WHAT TIME IT IS.

Time to shred.

fig. 4
"Forty-Eight Characters"
(Photo: TheLosAngelesDesignGroup)

use jokes is to try to think about breaking down the difference between architecture and its audience. Basically, asking the question: "How can buildings become more and more like the audience that observes them?" One experiment along those lines would be the project "Forty-Eight Characters" where we're casting balloon animals out of plaster. The balloon animals have all of these ludicrously suggestive, even lewd forms. What we want to do is make objects that solicit being touched in exactly the same way that bodies would offer themselves up to be touched. So it's a kind of joke, because they're exaggerated in the way that they're imitating a certain kind of physicality, but we want that joke to overcome the distance between people and things.

Another way in which we want to make jokes and play tricks is at the level of the discipline: what can we do to architecture that's funny? Those jokes have a way of helping us articulate limits and rules that we did not know existed until the joke was made. Just think about the questions you ask yourself when you hear a really cutting joke: "Is that funny?" and "Are they actually allowed to make a joke about that?" Another way to phrase those questions is that humor has revealed limit conditions in our thought. We may or may not be willing to actually transgress those limits. Maybe there are limits for a good reason, but at least the joke has shown us this boundary that we may not have been able to articulate before someone made the joke.

So that's what we want to do to architecture. "The Kid Gets Out of the

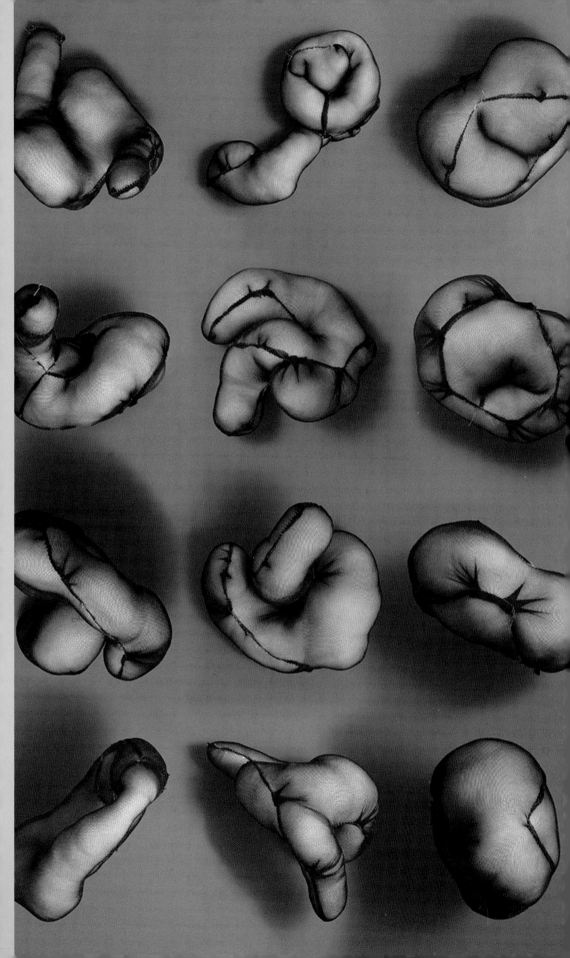

Picture" would be one of those jokes, and now I'm talking about the version in Los Angeles. One way to describe that project is to say that we filled an empty lot in Los Angeles with junk that is impersonating a building, and then we asked people to get in there and inhabit it as if it were a kind of building. I would say that's a kind of joke that we would hope provokes a deadly serious discussion. Are we allowed to do this? What can count as an architectural object and what can't? For instance, thinking about a stack of concrete masonry block—does that count as building or is that too low, is that still in the realm of a pile of construction material? What about concrete that's pretending to be fabric? Does that count? Is that allowed? What about the looseness of the assembly? What if it was very carefully made? What if there were these very tenuous or arbitrary connections between things? Of course we work very hard at producing tenuousness, but what we want to do is put it next to buildings of a kind of conventional type and construction and laugh a little bit nervously as we ask if this is allowed.

L: When you teach architecture and design to your students do you try to emphasize some of these experimental approaches like you were talking about earlier? How do you implant this kind of thing in someone who is still new to the field and learning? Have you seen any interesting results from this sort of education?

A: The first would be that I'm always trying to make students in my studios aware of the ideological structures that they are working inside. Every studio has a set of agendas beyond the impulse to make a building, and students should become experts in identifying what those agendas are. They should also be able to identify the beliefs held by their academic institution and what it thinks should be taught at a particular moment in time. I want students to be aware of those ideological contexts and also their historicity—that these are just beliefs that people have now, at this moment, in a very long history of beliefs. We always experience a moment in time as though the stuff we learn is fixed and true, but it has not always seemed fixed and true. It only seems that way now because a particular set of people won arguments over others. So I do what I can to expose my own beliefs and how they have shaped the project brief. That's one way—trying to become acutely aware of our position in history as much as possible.

The other way I do it is by pitting some of my own idiosyncratic design interests against the most conventional exercises that the discipline asks of us. For instance, how would you draw a plan differently if you weren't first thinking about the distribution of columns on a grid but instead arranged a series of whole parts up against one another, and then, *ex post facto*, had to rationalize how it stands up? Is there something at the core of what we do, like drawing a plan and thinking about how we produce space? Can you show how your way of doing that is different from other ways that we've seen in history? 🐇

Faux Documentation and Graphic Misbehavior

Joel Kerner

fig. 1 (facing)
Detail of "A-LOL," 2017

The production of construction documents is often perceived as one of the more banal obligations of architectural practice. They aren't given much attention in academic contexts, almost as if they are a necessary evil to execute the design intent. They exhibit an almost unintentional beauty in their layering of lines, notes, symbols, and dimensions, yet remain somewhat cold in their adherence to imposed standards such as Architectural Graphic Standards, National CAD Standards, or the CSI Uniform Drawing System. It is curious that practicing architects devote enormous effort toward the production of construction documents, yet the documents are rarely championed as exquisite artifacts of graphic achievement in the way that, say, hand drafting has been in the past, or digitally produced renderings are today. The following drawings contain a minefield of graphic misbehaviors, subverting the normative expectations of construction documents through composition, color, and visual flair.

The building represented in the drawing set "A-LOL" is a complete fabrication. It does not, and will not, exist in the physical world. However, the drawing set is annotated as if it were a genuine document for construction. Notational lines are directed to labels such as "Ferret Tickling Room" and "Cadaver Petting Zoo"; additional notes remind contractors to "Provide ADA accessible trap doors" and "Provide industrial grade W.C. to accommodate Taco Bell Customers." These drawings attempt to tease, charm, and vex the viewer with their irreverent alterations, much in the same way that urban graffiti toes the line between art and property damage.

The series of drawings entitled "Well, I Figured" takes a different approach to false documentation. Reminiscent of the early drawings of Thom Mayne, Neil Denari, and Wes Jones, these drawings are more sincere than cheeky. Unlike some practitioners today, Mayne, Denari, and Jones were interested in construction and the tangible execution of projects. As a result, their analytical drawings retained typical notational systems including structural grid lines, system labels, and view tags. Similarly, these drawings exhibit a disciplinary integrity in their adherence to known conventions of architectural documentation, yet they are nonetheless erroneous documents: the execution of the depicted designs is not contingent upon their two-dimensional graphic documentation. That is to say, digital fabrication has made the execution of these spaces quick and document-free.

Why create these drawings? In a way, they are part of an ongoing attempt to narrow the perceived gap between the academy and the profession, the polemical and the pragmatic, the speculators and the practitioners—you get the idea. They seek to find a common graphic ground between academics and practitioners by providing visual interest, while also teasing and departing from the seriousness and rigor of construction documentation. Through the intermingling of architectural documentation and graphic pop, the pseudo-documents presented here linger as an open-ended query into the methodologies and processes of architectural graphic production. 🐇

fig. 2 (facing)
"Well, I Figured," 2017

fig. 3-5 (following)
"A-LOL," 2017

fig. 6-11 (following)
"Well, I Figured," 2017

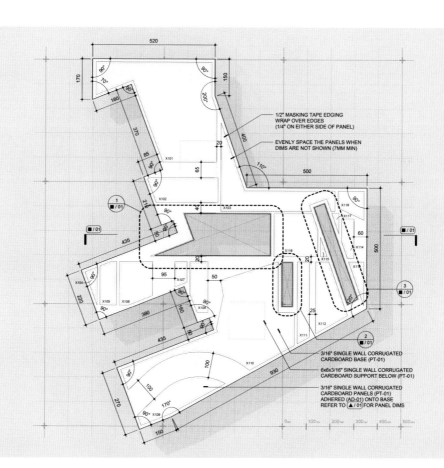

1/2" MASKING TAPE EDGING
WRAP OVER EDGES
(1/4" ON EITHER SIDE OF PANEL)

EVENLY SPACE THE PANELS WHEN
DIMS ARE NOT SHOWN (7MM MIN)

3/16" SINGLE WALL CORRUGATED
CARDBOARD BASE (PT-01)

6x6x3/16" SINGLE WALL CORRUGATED
CARDBOARD SUPPORT BELOW (PT-01)

3/16" SINGLE WALL CORRUGATED
CARDBOARD PANELS (PT-01)
ADHERED (AD-01) ONTO BASE
REFER TO (△/01) FOR PANEL DIMS

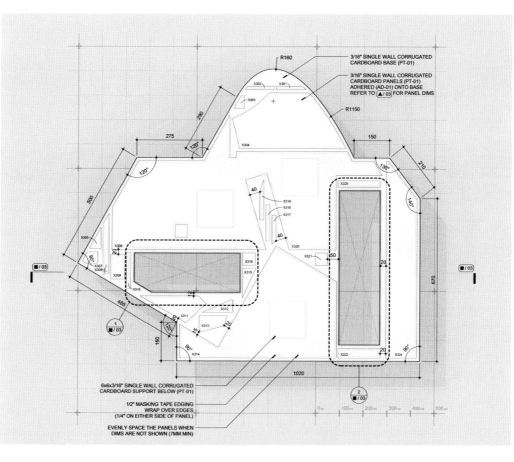

3/16" SINGLE WALL CORRUGATED
CARDBOARD BASE (PT-01)

3/16" SINGLE WALL CORRUGATED
CARDBOARD PANELS (PT-01)
ADHERED (AD-01) ONTO BASE
REFER TO (△/03) FOR PANEL DIMS

6x6x3/16" SINGLE WALL CORRUGATED
CARDBOARD SUPPORT BELOW (PT-01)

1/2" MASKING TAPE EDGING
WRAP OVER EDGES
(1/4" ON EITHER SIDE OF PANEL)

EVENLY SPACE THE PANELS WHEN
DIMS ARE NOT SHOWN (7MM MIN)

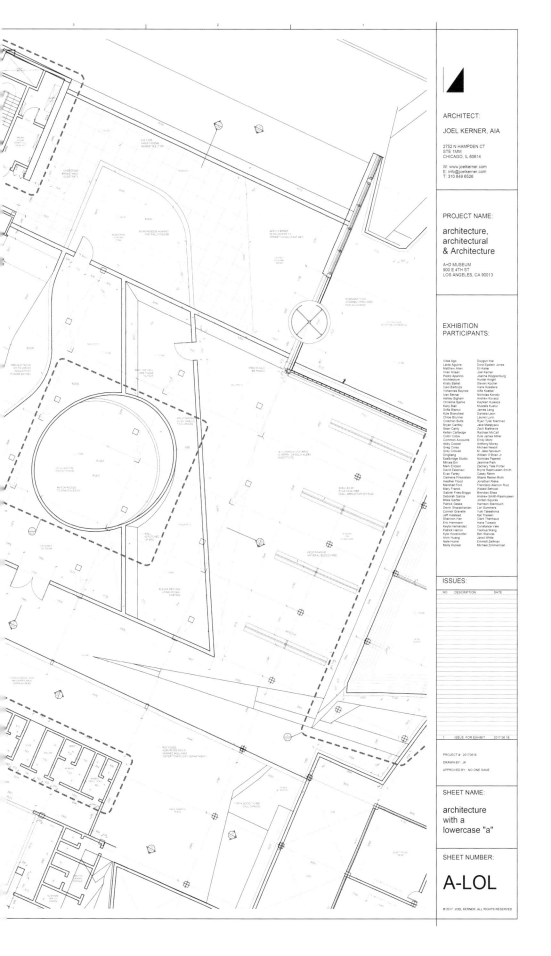

ARCHITECT:

JOEL KERNER, AIA

2752 N HAMPDEN CT
STE 1MM
CHICAGO, IL 60614

W: www.joelkerner.com
E: info@joelkerner.com
T: 310 849 6526

PROJECT NAME:

architecture,
architectural
& Architecture

A+D MUSEUM
900 E 4TH ST
LOS ANGELES, CA 90013

EXHIBITION
PARTICIPANTS:

Viola Ago	Duygun Inal
Laida Aguirre	Dora Epstein Jones
Matthew Allen	Eli Keller
Iman Ansari	Joel Kerner
Pedro Aparicio	Joanna Kloppenburg
Architecture	Hunter Knight
Kristy Balliet	Steven Kocher
Caio Barboza	Hans Koesters
Yohannes Bayines	Alfie Koetter
Ivan Bernal	Nicholas Korody
Ashley Bigham	Andrew Kovacs
Christina Bjerke	Kayleen Kuiesza
Kelly Blair	Mustafa Kustur
Sofia Blanco	James Leng
Kyle Branchesi	Daniela Leon
Chloe Brunner	Lauren Lynn
Coleman Butts	Ryan Tyler Martinez
Bryan Cantley	Jake Matalyaou
Sean Canfy	Zach Matthews
Kellan Cartledge	Rachael McCall
Colin Cobia	Kyle James Miller
Common Accounts	Emily Mohr
Abby Coover	Anthony Morey
Greg Corso	Michael Nesbit
Grey Crowell	M. Jake Newsum
Dingliang	William O'Brien Jr
Eastbridge Studio	Nicholas Papenski
Mircea Eri	Jasmine Park
Mark Ericson	Zachary Tate Porter
David Eskenazi	Bryné Rasmussen-Smith
Evan Farley	Casey Rehm
Clemens Finkelstein	Shane Reiner-Roth
Heather Flood	Jonathan Rieke
Marshall Ford	Francisco Alarcon Ruiz
Mary Franck	Walaild Sehwail
Gabriel Fries-Briggs	Brendan Shea
Deborah Garcia	Andrew Smith-Rasmussen
Miles Gertler	Jordan Squires
Patrick Geske	Harrison Steinbuch
Devin Gharakhanian	Lori Summers
Connor Gravelle	Yuki Takeshima
Jeff Halstead	Kat Thiesen
Shannon Han	Clark Thenhaus
Eric Herrmann	Haris Tursack
Keyla Hernandez	Constance Vale
Patrick Herron	Yachiua Wang
Kyle Hovenkotter	Ben Warwas
Alvin Huang	Jared White
Nate Hume	Emmett Zeitman
Molly Hunker	Michael Zimmerman

ISSUES:

NO	DESCRIPTION	DATE
1	ISSUE FOR EXHIBIT	2017.06.16

PROJECT #: 20170616

DRAWN BY: JK

APPROVED BY: NO ONE SANE

SHEET NAME:

architecture
with a
lowercase "a"

SHEET NUMBER:

A-LOL

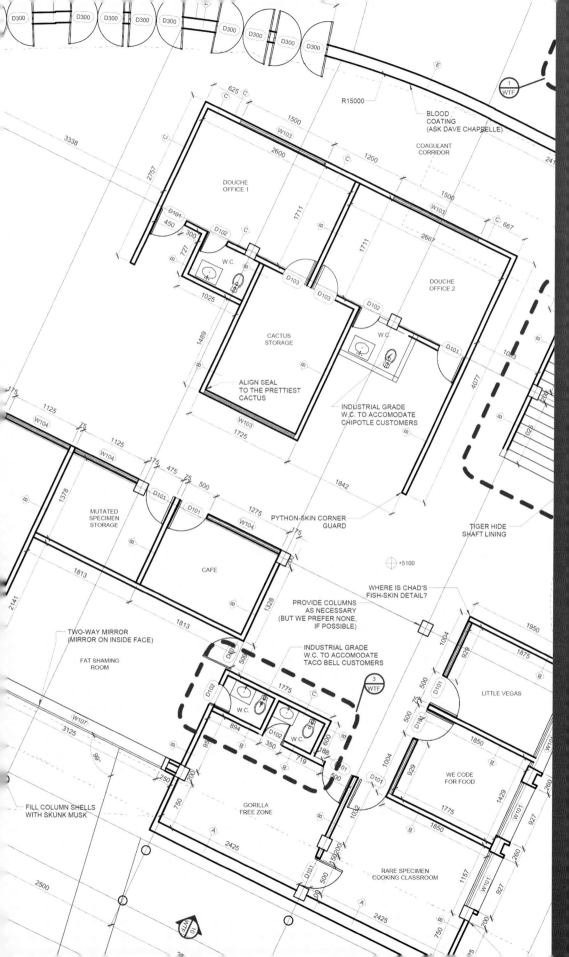

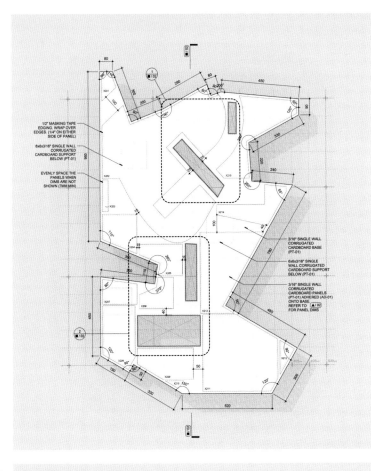

1/2" MASKING TAPE
EDGING. WRAP OVER
EDGES. (1/4" ON EITHER
SIDE OF PANEL)

6x6x3/16" SINGLE WALL
CARDBOARD SUPPORT
BELOW (PT-01)

EVENLY SPACE THE
PANELS WHEN
DIMS ARE NOT
SHOWN (7MM MIN)

3/16" SINGLE WALL
CORRUGATED
CARDBOARD BASE
(PT-01)

6x6x3/16" SINGLE
WALL CORRUGATED
CARDBOARD SUPPORT
BELOW (PT-01)

3/16" SINGLE WALL
CORRUGATED
CARDBOARD PANELS
(PT-01) ADHERED (AD-01)
ONTO BASE
REFER TO △/02
FOR PANEL DIMS

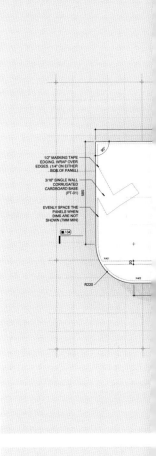

1/2" MASKING TAPE
EDGING. WRAP OVER
EDGES. (1/4" ON EITHER
SIDE OF PANEL)

3/16" SINGLE WALL
CORRUGATED
CARDBOARD BASE
(PT-01)

EVENLY SPACE THE
PANELS WHEN
DIMS ARE NOT
SHOWN (7MM MIN)

R220

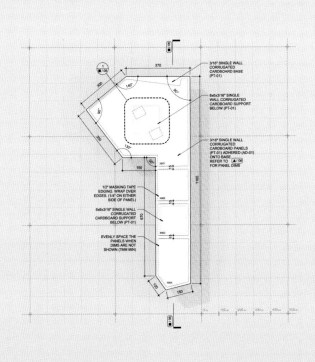

3/16" SINGLE WALL
CORRUGATED
CARDBOARD BASE
(PT-01)

6x6x3/16" SINGLE
WALL CORRUGATED
CARDBOARD SUPPORT
BELOW (PT-01)

3/16" SINGLE WALL
CORRUGATED
CARDBOARD PANELS
(PT-01) ADHERED (AD-01)
ONTO BASE
REFER TO △/06
FOR PANEL DIMS

1/2" MASKING TAPE
EDGING. WRAP OVER
EDGES. (1/4" ON EITHER
SIDE OF PANEL)

6x6x3/16" SINGLE WALL
CORRUGATED
CARDBOARD SUPPORT
BELOW (PT-01)

EVENLY SPACE THE
PANELS WHEN
DIMS ARE NOT
SHOWN (7MM MIN)

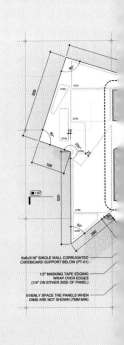

6x6x3/16" SINGLE WALL CORRUGATED
CARDBOARD SUPPORT BELOW (PT-01)

1/2" MASKING TAPE EDGING.
WRAP OVER EDGES.
(1/4" ON EITHER SIDE OF PANEL)

EVENLY SPACE THE PANELS WHEN
DIMS ARE NOT SHOWN (7MM MIN)

6x6x3/16" SINGLE WALL CORRUGATED CARDBOARD SUPPORT BELOW (PT-01)

3/16" SINGLE WALL CORRUGATED CARDBOARD PANELS (PT-01) ADHERED (AD-01) ONTO BASE REFER TO ▲/04 FOR PANEL DIMS

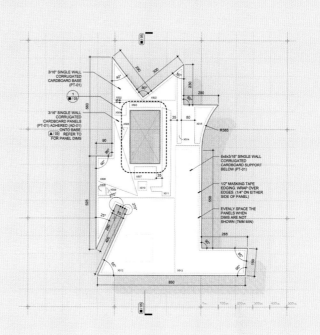

3/16" SINGLE WALL CORRUGATED CARDBOARD BASE

3/16" SINGLE WALL CORRUGATED CARDBOARD PANELS (PT-01) ADHERED (AD-01) ONTO BASE REFER TO ▲/05 FOR PANEL DIMS

6x6x3/16" SINGLE WALL CORRUGATED CARDBOARD SUPPORT BELOW (PT-01)

1/2" MASKING TAPE EDGING. WRAP OVER EDGES. (1/4" ON EITHER SIDE OF PANEL)

EVENLY SPACE THE PANELS WHEN DIMS ARE NOT SHOWN (7MM MIN)

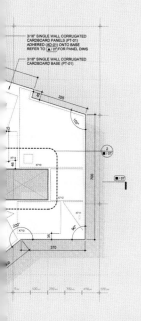

3/16" SINGLE WALL CORRUGATED CARDBOARD PANELS (PT-01) ADHERED (AD-01) ONTO BASE REFER TO ▲/07 FOR PANEL DIMS

3/16" SINGLE WALL CORRUGATED CARDBOARD BASE (PT-01)

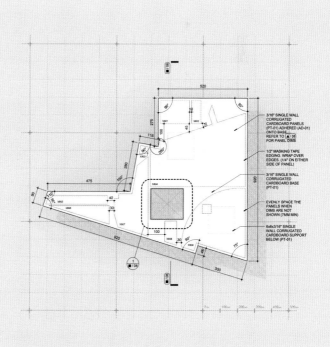

3/16" SINGLE WALL CORRUGATED CARDBOARD PANELS (PT-01) ADHERED (AD-01) ONTO BASE REFER TO ▲/08 FOR PANEL DIMS

1/2" MASKING TAPE EDGING. WRAP OVER EDGES. (1/4" ON EITHER SIDE OF PANEL)

3/16" SINGLE WALL CORRUGATED CARDBOARD BASE (PT-01)

EVENLY SPACE THE PANELS WHEN DIMS ARE NOT SHOWN (7MM MIN)

6x6x3/16" SINGLE WALL CORRUGATED CARDBOARD SUPPORT BELOW (PT-01)

The Remarkable Lost Projects of the U.S. Army Corps

Kristi Cheramie and Matthew Seibert

Atop the most accessible pile are transcribed notes from an October 1928 meeting at the Vicksburg District Office. The notes record attendance of the Commander of the Mississippi Valley Division, several engineers from Atchafalaya Basin Levee District, and a young engineer named Eugene Davis. Written in shorthand and missing the third of four pages, the notes allude to the formation of The Office of Recovery and Reconciliation (ORR) and to its twofold mission: to measure the loss of cultural heritage due to the Great Flood of 1927, and to develop a plan that would prevent comparable cultural losses during future flood events. The last page of notes details the official charge to Davis, assigning him exclusive management of the office due to his "unique, eccentric reading of infrastructure as the potential mediator between memory and secure futures."

Following the meeting notes are the only remaining documents (personal accounts, private correspondence, and official transactions) of Davis's nearly forgotten efforts to question the role infrastructure plays in the shared perception of place. These papers expose the socio-political climate within which the Army Corps operated and reflect the nation's struggle to find control, peace, and stability. The works of the Office of Recovery and Reconciliation are a direct response to the Great Flood of 1927, and a counterpoint to what was otherwise an unprecedented era of decision-making about the design and management of the American landscape.

We, the authors, were given access to ORR's files in 2013 and now present a selection of the documents to you, the reader, along with our notes, taken while piecing together the story of the lost projects of the U.S. Army Corps of Engineers.

13 JULY 2013

OFR - 28 - 01

- Who is Eugene Davis?
   from Morganza, LA or .. ?

   BORN 1903
   1 VICKSBURG, MI
   SEE USACE EMPLOYMEN
   RECORDS FROM 1925.

- Why was OFR founded? Any budget
  allocation in Flood Control Act of 1928?
  OFR oversight: located in which
      department / division?

      DEPT. OF
      REAL ESTATE

- WHERE is complete archive stored?
  How to we get access?

- "PUBLIC SPACES OF CULTURAL CONSERVATION"

7/
4/6

COPY

Genealogical Register

List of Bodies Moved From The Site of St. Ann Cemetery in the Morganza
Floodway, Pointe Coupee Parish.

UNITED STATES ARMY CORPS OF ENGINEERS
MISSISSIPPI VALLEY DIVISION
ATCHAFALAYA BASIN LEVEE DISTRICT
MORGANZA, LOUISIANA

OFFICE OF
RECOVERY AND RECONCILIATION

3 December 1928

Mission Statement:

To directly engage the public engineering endeavors of the Mississippi Valley
Division; to mediate the confluence of flows between time, space, and
infrastructure; to intensify the joy and confront the suffering of communities,
families, and individuals who reside in the Lower Mississippi Basin; to prevent
future loss of cultural memory due to environmental destruction.

Objectives:

(1) Document ecological and cultural processes throughout the District, with
particular attention to their intersection or overlap.

(2) Identify, collect, catalog and curate evidence of material culture related to
flood events at multiple scales of space and time.

(3) Appropriate residual spaces within Army Corps control structures for storage,
laboratory, and curation.

(4) Facilitate continuity of cultural memory by identifying totemic objects and
actions throughout the Lower Basin and designing public spaces of cultural
conservation.

Essayons,

Eugene Davis

ED:jc
Encl. (2)

H-28 · I-28 · J-28

H-29 · I-29 · J-

I-30 · I-30

I-30

I-31

17 SEPT 1951

Excavation and precast concrete piling for gated portion of Morganza Control
No. DA-16-047-eng-G27 dated 18 May 1950, with Raymond Concrete Pile Co.,
DA-16-047-eng-840 dated 14 August 1950 with Farnsworth & Chambers Co.,
Steel reinforcing rods in place for gated portion of supers...

CORPS OF ENGINEERS, U. S. ARMY, NEW OR
MORGANZA CONTROL ST.

MORGANZA

ORR - PROJECT 2B MAP

- who is presenting w/ Eugene?
- Map outlines 6 projects for
- Atchafalaya Basin - any
  under construction yet?

- Projects mapped:
  - MELVILLE CREVASSE Chapel
  - Old River Stilling Collection
  - Morganza Baffle Blocks Tomb
  - Memorial to the lost Village
  - Simmesport Fuse Plug Project

- LOGBOOKS SF
  SKETCHES FOI
  MELVILLE CR
  CHAPEL (19

- E.D.'S CALE
  SHOWS "SIT
  SURVEYS: N
  03-12 FEB 19

Project 46TT-02: TRIBUTE TOWERS

1946?

Monitoring towers designed for
Vicksburg ACoE headquarters

appear to be formal interpriations
of Fisk's valley borings from
1944 survey
- Check Fisk archive
@ LSU (reference to
Eugene?)

Never realized?

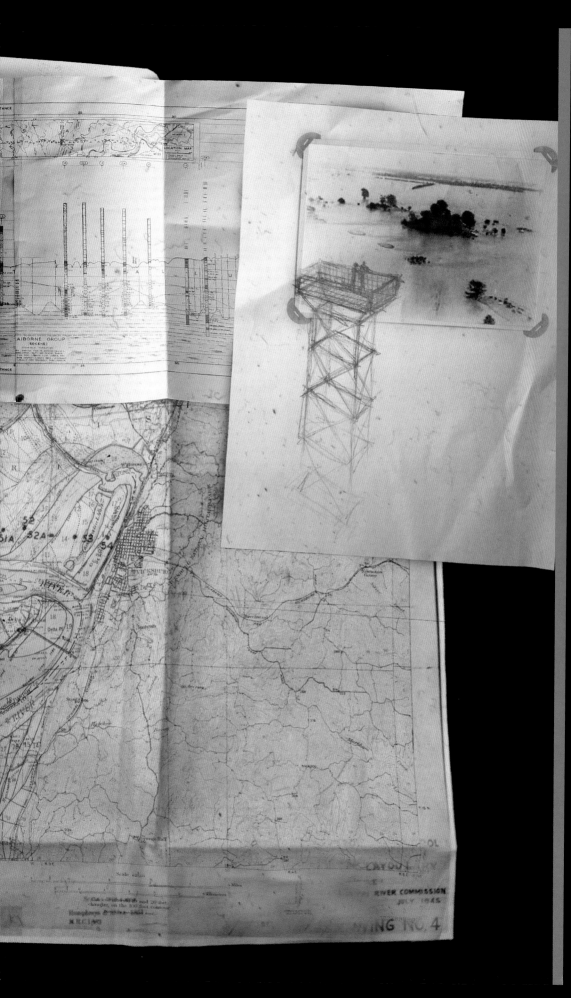

CORPS OF ENGINEERS

Project Objectives

- Provide the ability to occupy space of levee break

- The intention is not to erase evidence of devastation, but rather memorialize it

- Create a 'chapel' to remember the people, possessions, and places lost to the flood; hold events in memory

- Recognize the degree of subservience to clear water

- Pay homage to the power of the river

CORPS OF ENGINEERS, U. S. ARMY
OFFICE OF THE PRESIDENT, MISSISSIPPI RIVER COMMISSION
VICKSBURG, MISSISSIPPI

Office of Situational Preparedness

CREVASSE CHAPEL
Section and Details

DRAWING NO. 23

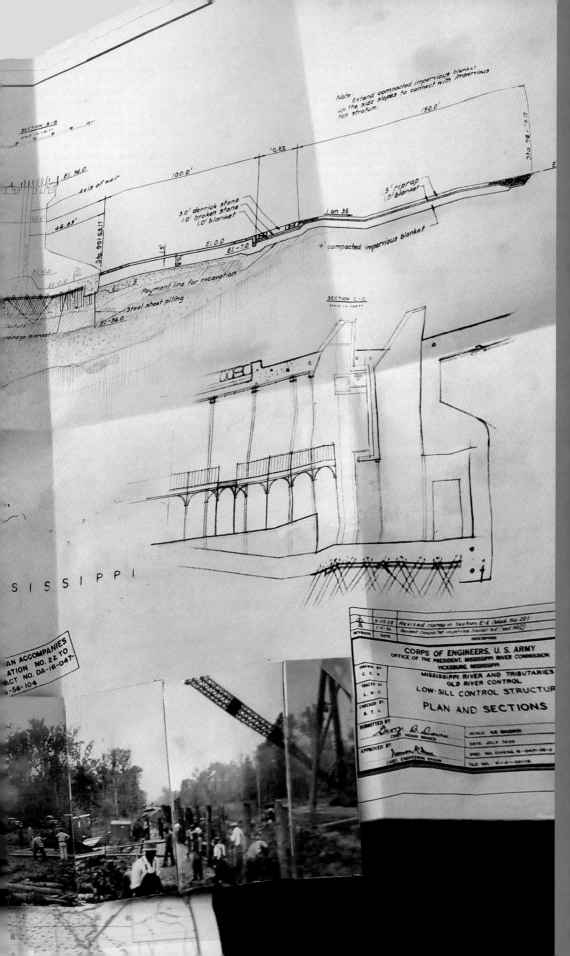

SECTION B-B
SCALE IN FEET

Axis of weir

EL 34.0

100.0'

25.0'

150.0'

Note: Extend compacted impervious blanket up the side slopes to connect with impervious top stratum.

46.83'

Sta. 991+63.17

3.0' derrick stone
1.0' broken stone
1.0' blanket

1 on 35

5' riprap
1.0' blanket

EL 0.0

EL -7.0

4' compacted impervious blanket

EL 0.0

EL -11.5

Payment line for excavation

Steel sheet piling

EL -36.0

drainage blanket

SECTION C-C
SCALE IN FEET

S S I S S I P P I

9-15-58   Revised riprap in Section E-E (Mod. No. 28)
2-14-56   Revised compacted impervious blanket and [   ]
REVISION   DATE   DESCRIPTION

CORPS OF ENGINEERS, U. S. ARMY
OFFICE OF THE PRESIDENT, MISSISSIPPI RIVER COMMISSION
VICKSBURG, MISSISSIPPI

MISSISSIPPI RIVER AND TRIBUTARIES
OLD RIVER CONTROL
LOW-SILL CONTROL STRUCTUR

PLAN AND SECTIONS

DRAWN BY
C.C.S.
TRACED BY
L.R.C.
CHECKED BY
A.T.L.
SUBMITTED BY
APPROVED BY

SCALE AS SHOWN
DATE JULY 1955

From: **Cheramie, Kristi** cheramie.1@osu.edu
Subject: USACE: ORR Materials request
Date: February 03, 2018 at 1:00 PM
To: Wingate, Mark wingate@usace.army.mil
Cc: mseibert@ccny.cuny.edu

Dear Mr. Wingate,

Thank you for supporting our research related to the history of USACE's Office of Recovery and Reconciliation over the last few years. Your staff has kindly made the requested folder of materials available for review and documentation. This has enabled us to move ahead with the first in a series of articles on the lost history of the ORR.

We are now writing to request permission to access the complete archive of the Office. It is our understanding that the archive contains additional models, construction drawing sets, log books and miscellaneous items from ORR's head engineer, Eugene Davis. We are basing our request on a document contained in the first folder: a finding aid, dated January, 1968, which most likely corresponds to the decommissioning of ORR and subsequent removal of all materials to the archive. See attached for a scan of the finding aid.

It is our hope to gain access to these materials, with permission to photograph or scan individual items.

Thank you again for your continued support and please don't hesitate to contact me or Matthew directly with any questions.

Respectfully,
Kristi

kristi cheramie
associate professor
undergraduate studies chair, landscape archit
austin e. knowlton school of architecture
ohio state university

Finding Aid:
Office of Recovery and Reconciliation

JANUARY 19

1. ORGANIZATIONAL DOCUMENTS
   a. Office of Recovery and Reconciliation Mission Statement. 1928
   b. Correspondence. Levee Boards and ORR. 1929
   c. Photo Album. Documentation of 1927 flood with notes. 1928

2. PROJECT 46TT-02: TRIBUTE TOWERS   1931-46
   a. Site Plans Map. District Headquarters:
      New Orleans, La; Vicksburg, Ms; Memphis, Tn; Little Rock, Ak.
   b. Vicksburg Plan Map. Historic river channels and soil borings.
   c. Vicksburg Section Elevation
      NOTE: Fisk soil borings augmented as monitoring / tribute towers
   d. Tower Sketch Collage. 1927 flood image with hand drawn towers
   e. Traveling Model Box.
      'Unfolding' wooden model fabricated out of machinist's toolbox.
      5"x12"x10", wood.
         i. hand sketches
         ii. 1927 flood photographs

3. PROJECT 29SC-A: THE STILLING COLLECTION 1929-6
   a. Plan and Section, Construction Document.
      Half of control structure; symmetrical.
   b. Sections, Construction Document. Details of control structure.
   c. Photomontage Panoramas (3).
      Documentation of construction underway.
   d. Photo Binder
      Documentation of construction of Old River control structure.
   e. Traveling Model Box.
      'Unfolding' wooden model showing underground baffle block stru

17 SEPT 1967   CORPS OF ENGINEERS, U. S. ARMY, NEW ORLEANS DISTRICT   NO. 8845-5
OLD RIVER CONTROL HEADQUARTERS

Corps Officers from the Vicksburg and New Orleans District Offices gather at the Old River Control Headquarters to discuss the termination of the Office of Recovery and Reconciliation due to recent controversy surrounding the ORR's current project (Project AO.5113-0). ORR Head Engineer Eugene Davis (center) presents formal arguments against termination. ORR is given one month to decommission all ongoing projects and move all materials to the archives of the New Orleans District Office.

fig. 7 (facing)
Email correspondence between authors and Mark Wingate, Deputy District Engineer for Project Management, New Orleans District Office of the U.S. Army Corps of Engineers.

fig. 8
Photograph (U.S. Army Corps of Engineers, New Orleans District Office Archive).

In 1967, after almost 40 years of solitary work and limited progress, Davis was again summoned to meet with District Officers from the Mississippi Valley Division. This time, on the heels of his most controversial proposal, which sought to balance components of flood control infrastructure with measures of human loss and ecological disturbance, the tone of the meeting was markedly different. Davis was given one month to dismantle ORR and decommission all projects. Records of the office were discretely moved to the New Orleans District Office, where they remained untouched and largely forgotten until 2013.

Remarkably, amid an atmosphere of outwardly assured technological supremacy, the lost documents of the Office of Recovery and Reconciliation reveal an institution divided over how to manage floods and the national anxieties that accompany them. Exposing concern for the consequences of engineering the mighty Mississippi, these documents speak to an alternate version of the Army Corps, one willing to wrestle with the costs of its unprecedented reach for power and control.

Full of unmapped gaps and spatial aberrations, the documents construct a mythic topology of competing histories and counterfactual possibilities for the Lower Mississippi basin. Positioned at the slippage between documented truths, unfinished business, and mythic tales, these materials dissolve obvious markers of past and present, found and fabricated, and expose an institution's quixotic desire for permanence in the face of constant change. 🐇

Title Pending Your Consideration

Kate Lipkowitz

fig. 1 (facing)
Harry Weese Cheese
(Image: Kate Lipkowitz)

One afternoon last fall I glimpsed an inventory of studio projects that critic Luis Pancorbo Crespo was making in advance of a review. In it he distilled each project into a single word. My own project, a museum for early aviation experimentation nestled in the woods overlooking the Potomac, he dubbed "The Fuselodge."

When asked about the list, he continued to sketch, explaining that the public practice of nicknaming buildings is an inevitability beyond the control of the designer and something we might grow accustomed to sooner rather than later. His own Vegas Altas Congress Center, an award-winning building designed in collaboration with faculty member Inés Martín Robles, is known by locals as "SpongeBob."

How might designers begin to interpret a nickname? Is it a badge of honor, or a horror unto architecture? When asked, Martín Robles waves a hand at SpongeBob, and brings a more surprising example to light. The duo designed several blocks of low income transitional housing for the municipality of Parla several kilometers south of Madrid. As the buildings were erected, narrow interior compartments comprising the individual units were exposed prior to the construction of the façade. Members of the surrounding community grimly nicknamed the apartments "mausoleums." Yet Martín Robles is cool and collected regarding the moniker. She argues that the nickname is an important part of the public engagement and understanding of architecture. It represents public curiosity about a project and an effort to understand

fig. 2 (following)
Ekuan View Master
(Image: Kate Lipkowitz)

fig. 3 (above)
104 Temporary Dwellings in Parla, Madrid
(Image: Luis Pancorbo Crespo)

it. Furthermore, she states that a building that cannot be approached in this way has in a sense failed, and that all student projects should pass the one-word summation test.

This is not a case for so-called "ducks" in the Venturian sense,[1] however. Pancorbo Crespo cites ETSAM professor Antonio Miranda, who makes an apt and biting criticism of buildings that express their intentions all too literally in their form, calling them "porno architecture." Miranda feels that there is something crude about these buildings both commercially and artistically. Still, if we as designers can muster a fraction of the even-keeled sensibility of Pancorbo Crespo and Martín Robles toward such uninvited monikers, the phenomenon of nicknaming might provide us with some larger lessons about public engagement with architecture.

These nicknames might be more upsetting to the duo if it were a singular phenomenon, but theirs is hardly the first building to acquire a less-than-desirable sobriquet. In fact, theirs isn't even the only building to receive a SpongeBob comparison. In their book *O-14: Projection and Reception*, Reiser and Umemoto open the chapter "Comedic Typology" with a collage depicting the O-14 tower under construction and one SpongeBob SquarePants. They then reveal that the same project has been likened to a termite mound, Melnikov's House, a wind tower, and a laundry basket.

To account for these comparisons, Reiser and Umemoto liken the

1
Robert Venturi, Denise Scott Brown, and Steven Izenour, *Learning from Las Vegas: The Forgotten Symbolism of Architectural Form* (Cambridge: MIT Press, 1977).

fig. 4 (above)
The Altas Congress Center, A.K.A.
"SpongeBob"
(Image: Kate Lipkowitz)

2
Jesse Reiser and Nanako Umemoto,
O-14: Projection and Reception, ed.
Brett Steele (London: Architectural
Association, 2012), 41-2.

3
Ibid, 47.

O-14 tower to Chauncey "Chance" Gardner, played by Peter Sellers in the film *Being There*. Chance, they say, "is an empty cipher, [whom] everyone thinks speaks metaphorically and projects a deep profundity into whatever he says, all the while revealing more about themselves (the context) than dumb Chauncey."[2] An important thing to keep in mind is that the nickname might say more about the person that bestows it than about the building.

In exploring why people might be driven to nickname particular buildings, the architects borrow a term from music criticism, suggesting that architecture is replete with "unconsummated symbols." In music, this means that some of the gestures within a composition have a resonance or seeming symbolism beyond the immediate notes and chords, and that this symbolism then exists in a state of "virtual indeterminacy." It is "as if we know that there is (or rather, has to be) some meaning, without ever being able to establish what that meaning is."[3] For me, this calls to mind the character Oedipa Maas in Pynchon's *The Crying of Lot 49*. So keen is her nose for symbolism, so apt is she to notice symbols everywhere, that we are not sure if she is hot on the trail of a vast conspiracy or if she has descended into a kind of schizophrenic madness.

There is something very believable about this notion that architectural symbols have a virtual indeterminacy. The gestures a building makes and their emotive properties can certainly elicit a response similar to music.

fig. 5 (above)
Lina Bo Bardi Crab
(Image: Kate Lipkowitz)

It is no stretch to say that people are inclined to seek out symbols and draw associations, given that schema are a basic principle in cognitive science. But what do *Being There* or *The Crying of Lot 49* have to do with SpongeBob? Do these fictional examples really have any correlation with real world outcomes? Sure, the public is bound to draw associations, but is the public actually trained to expect or pursue symbols in architecture? Certainly not in the way professionals are.

When it comes to what generates a nickname, Martín Robles's observation that it represents an attempt to understand the structure is most astute. One fundamental rule governing the bestowal of nicknames seems to be an absurdity grounded in a visual observation or cue. Nicknames like "The Gherkin" for the Swiss Re building or "SpongeBob" for the Congress Center distill large and complex projects into comprehensible and friendly figures. There is an irresistible dual quality to them: they have both wit and naiveté. This is not to say that such nicknames are without a critical quality, but I wish to distinguish them from a second category of more pointed cultural critique.

Here the visual association is the dominant trend helping us to understand the formulation of the building. My own illustration of

Kenji Ekuan's Metabolist ski lodge demonstrates this point—this kind of playful visual free association has the ability to bring into focus a larger architectural concept. For me the ski lodge is none other than the 3D View Master (fig. 2). Ekuan, who is most famous for the design of the Kikkoman soy sauce bottle, operates within the framework of the Japanese Metabolists, who experimented with compact and theoretically mass producible forms. The look and feel of this project calls to mind that particular toy for a reason. It grows out of the same era and ideas about production.

There is another dimension in which a nickname derived from a visual cue becomes a critique of the architecture; not as a critique of the particular work, but insofar as the work of architecture exists as a part of a larger system. In other words, the nickname can be a political or social critique. Under this lens the nickname "mausoleum" given to the temporary housing project is less a critique of the individual building than it is a manifestation of a larger problem of urban development coupled with economic hardship. The morbid theme speaks not only to a visual association, but to larger associations and experience of a world community in the process of contracting both spatially and financially.

Architecture is ripe for precisely this kind of criticism by association because of the forces driving its creation. Corporations, institutions, and governments are the major benefactors or instigators of architecture. In a sense, the friendly absurdity of calling the Swiss Re building "The Gherkin" might be a more pointed critique alluding to the surreal scale of large financial institutions both in our figurative and literal landscapes. It could also be a reflection of the sublime enormity of the thing paired with an absolute opacity and lack of understanding by the general public regarding the functions such institutions perform.

Perhaps the nickname acts most strongly when it has these dual dimensions. An important case-in-point is the China Central Television or CCTV building in Beijing. Here is a building with an outstanding pedigree: it sits in a major world capital, represents one of the largest media organizations in the world, and is designed by the offices of OMA. The irony of the CCTV acronym will not be lost on anyone who follows the news concerning Chinese state media politics. The building, it has been noted, looks like a large pair of pants. Consequently, it has come to be known as dà kùchǎ (大裤衩), or the big boxer shorts.

In response, state media proposed other official names for the building; however, they couldn't stanch the flow of absurdist nicknames. The Chinese language by virtue of its structure elevates the pun to a level far beyond the capabilities of English. Each proposed name for the structure was met with an equally devastating homophonic retort. One proposed name for the building was zhīchuāng (知窗) meaning "the window of knowledge." Some members of the public then referred to the building as a zhìchuāng (痔疮) or "hemorrhoid," which could be pure irreverence or might suggest that the building encapsulates a sort of grotesque allegory about state-run media. In this most confrontational form the nickname has extended beyond its initial visual association and its inherent criticism is laid bare. It becomes apparent that the nickname has little if anything to do with the building itself and everything to do with what it represents. The loosely scatological approach is a rebellion to counter the seriousness of the institution housed there.

Opposite this example is one that's funny on the surface and dismally lacking in depth by comparison. Adjacent to the aforementioned Gherkin and not far from the Cheese Grater (so named for its visual similarity to the common culinary item) is a project under construction that has been celebrated by the developers as "Canned Ham." This comparison led critic John Metcalf to mock the "pairing reminiscent of a Cuban sandwich" and question what culinary catastrophe might be the next imposition on the London skyline. Here the seemingly inevitable corporate commodification of the nickname game reduces the notion of public perception to mere kitsch. This is a different kind of "duck," one that does not manifest the function of the structure, but instead co-opts and attempts to direct the public response to a structure in a way that is perhaps more pernicious than CCTV's attempts at rebranding. By comparison it is profoundly unsatisfying. In this light, we might grow to love and understand the nickname: it only really works when it's a little mischievous. 🐇

IT'S THAT TIME AGAIN.

Rip this page to pieces; toss at nearby newlyweds.

(nearly got him that time...)

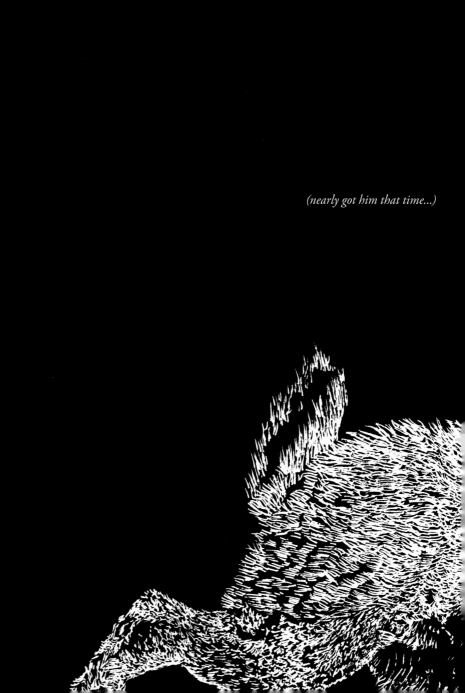

"A Mass Outpouring of Love": A Chat with *Planet Earth II: Cities* Producer Fredi Devas

The Editors

Kirk (L): While ideas of urban ecology and the urban wild have been discussed in the scientific and design communities since the 1970s, the long-standing tradition within nature documentary films has been to intentionally remove all elements of civilization and the human, in order to capture the wonders of the natural world in their pure and untarnished form. So I find it actually quite revolutionary for a platform such as *Planet Earth*, arguably the most influential nature program of the past 20 years, to break away from the expectations of its viewers and to present its plant and animal subjects in such an anthropogenic context. The city is presented to global mainstream audiences as an equally rich and dynamic habitat for any number of vibrant ecologies. Can you talk about this decision and what drew you to producing this particular episode?

Fredi (F): Well, my background is in desert ecology, actually, and the challenges animals face living in extreme xeric environments. So when I was brought on to the *Planet Earth II* team, I think everyone was quite keen that I should work on the desert show. But when I heard there would be an episode exploring cities, I really jumped on that, because I feel that it's an incredibly important issue to talk about. How does the human species relate to wildlife given that over half of us now live in the urban context, and that that context, as you mentioned, has only recently been described as a potential habitat for nonhuman species in the first place?

Filming the episode was incredibly different, and difficult. You can't just wake up and say, "Okay, let's take the Jeep out. What are we filming today?" There's a lot of intense planning that is required, and lots of paper work and bureaucracy to sort through.

L: It must have been interesting during the planning process to have to take on the logic of these other species in order to follow them through the city. In particular, it was fascinating to watch the monkey scenes, because they use the architecture of the city in ways that are just so completely different than the way we humans use it. It makes you realize that we may not really be using our architecture to its full potential. I'm curious what strategies or planning you undertook to follow these creatures through the urban tapestry given their various modes of travel.

F: Yes, that was key with the monkeys, with both the langurs in Jodhpur and the macaques in Jaipur. They're just running across the canopy, up on top of all the roofs and jumping between buildings. And for langurs, a six-meter jump is pretty straightforward, even for the little ones. So that was really difficult, because when a fight broke out elsewhere, we'd have to run down five flights of stairs to get to street level, search around for where they went, knock on a stranger's door and say, "Please, can we run through your house to your rooftop to film some monkeys that we think are there?" And we'd often get up there, then have to go, "Thank you very much, we're gonna run back down now." And put on our shoes, and back on the street we'd go. It was manic. But eventually we came to know that the females were staying static in a particular area, and that the fighters would often revolve around the dominant females' tree. So we'd base ourselves near the females in the morning, and the fight would tend to circle back to us at some point.

But what is interesting, also, is that you just can't see the animals as you're walking, so you end up having to rely a lot on sounds. Langur males, for instance, love to make noise. So they go to places with corrugated iron roofs, or they'll find massive metal signs, and they'll jump off the metal to create this really powerful reverberation. We were filming near one spot that had a lot of weddings, and Indian weddings tend to feature lots of music, particularly high brassy instruments and drumming. And when the music would play, the bachelor male langurs would just go nuts, and would run towards it then back to their spots to make their own sounds. It was fascinating to watch them use the architectural material in such a way.

If there's one story I really want to explore through film, it's the way in which animals use architecture to enhance features of the natural world that might not otherwise be enhanced. There's this one little frog, for instance, that goes inside the tunnels under motorways to call for females. In there that one little croak can sound incredibly loud and travel great distances. I love the idea that there are all these opportunities to amplify one's communication or behavior. Lizards using lamps or asphalt to warm up, for instance, or animals using reflective surfaces in various ways. There are many examples of particular species of birds now

singing at different times to strategically avoid the noise of rush hour traffic, even though those times are not necessarily the time at which they vocalize in the wild. So while there's plenty of examples of animals adapting to urban challenges, I'm particularly interested in animals who've found ways to amplify their lives in the urban context.

L: Yes, as we strive to design hyper-inclusive, multi-species urban spaces, it's so interesting to think through what are often accidental similarities between architectures of the city and architectures of, let's say, the forest. Like when the monkeys are climbing up and down the powerlines, very much the way they use vines. It would be fascinating to start documenting the formal echoes between the two worlds, and how animals have started to take advantage of potentials we normally wouldn't even think to notice. There seems to be so much design inspiration at the places where different species logics or species "cultures" overlap.

But as we see with the monkeys, this can also be the site of quite a bit of antagonism—where resources and space and the appropriate use of particular spaces is highly contested. With monkeys invading various spaces and stealing food and belongings from people (without any notion of what's "polite"), I'm curious what you observed in regards to the mutual respect that is still forged within these antagonistic relationships. I know in India much of the respect and care for monkeys is rooted in local religion, and

I'm curious whether you think these types of intimate symbioses can be transplanted or fostered in cities with completely different sociocultural contexts.

F: Yes, that's a big question, and a good question. To start, I guess—if you look at the difference between langurs and macaques, straight away you can see that one is very easy to tolerate in your city, and the other is less so. The Indian people are like no other people, in my opinion, in that they are extraordinary at accepting animals into their cities. They are so tolerant, it's amazing. Both the macaques and the langurs are associated with Lord Hanuman, who among other things led an army of monkeys to defeat the forces of evil in the Battle of Lanka. Yet while they're both associated, the langurs are more closely associated with Hanuman than the macaques. Langurs are very regal creatures. If you have a handful of peanuts, and you extend it towards them, there might grow a little queue of langurs, of different sizes, who will each wait their turn. One will literally hold your hand in one hand and pick a peanut out of it, one at a time, have a seat with it, maybe grab another, then hop off the wall, and the next one takes its turn. It's the most orderly primate feeding I've ever witnessed! It's extraordinary, and so polite.

Whereas with the macaques, they'll hastily grab all the peanuts they can, bear their teeth, and look at you in a totally distrustful manner—it's a totally different experience. It's frightening, even. Even though

fig. 4

Lenny's been hustling for years, but lately he's fallen out of love with his craft. "The smartphone generation have made it too easy," he says. "I can score three or four sodas in an hour, and nobody even *notices* me. Where is the drama?! This job used to take guile. It used to demand skill. Now? Pfft."

Lenny says that many of his friends in the community are struggling to find meaning in their work these days. "I don't even drink them anymore, you know. The sodas, I mean. It's just too sad."

(Photo: BBC/*Planet Earth II*)

langurs are bigger, stronger, have larger teeth, and are potentially more dangerous, their temperament is just so placid, usually. It's not always the case, of course. There's one park in Jodhpur, Mandore Gardens, where there's this massive troupe of about 70 langurs, and they've got into a few bad habits, and can get a bit gnarly. But generally, the other langurs around Jodhpur that I saw were extremely well-behaved in human terms.

So I think there's always going to be certain animals that we're more tolerant of in our cities, or happy to share space with. And the reasons for this can be quite strange at times. You can observe, for instance, very strange aesthetic preferences for certain animals—people love red squirrels in Britain and don't think much of gray squirrels. It's quite an abstract prejudice that they've gotten into their heads. The more beautiful the bird the more likely it is to be offered a bird feeder. So of course there are human preferences for what we see as lovely and what we see as vermin. Squirrels versus rats is an obvious one—one has a bushy tail, the other doesn't. One has a reputation for frequenting more "dirty" places, and so on, so yes, there are lots of examples where human aesthetics plays a major role.

But ultimately, I think a major factor in convincing people to welcome animals into their cities in more intentional ways has to do with the mental health benefits. There are a number of induced stress studies where people are, you know, given a hard math test to complete in a

short amount of time or something. A panel of people will then give the participant negative feedback on how they've done, causing people's heart rates and cortisol levels to spike. Those people are then given the option to sit in a lobby with soothing music or take a walk in a park. And as you might expect, people's heart rates decrease significantly faster in the park. Further, they've done studies comparing low biodiversity parks, with a lawn and a few old trees, and high biodiversity parks, with lots of heterogeneous plantings, and the high biodiversity parks have all kinds of supplemental effects. It works with pictures, even, which shows that its really more about a kind of perceived biodiversity. A picture of a bunch of birds swimming will have a more positive effect than a photo of a single bird. So if we walk into an environment, even a simple one, and perceive it as biologically complex, it can have enormous effects on our mental well-being.

L: Yes, I'm curious if you've ever read the book *How Forests Think* by Eduardo Kohn? Kohn is an anthropologist working with the Runa people in Ecuador, and he approaches much of his work through Saussure and semiology. And at one point he gives this really intimate account of a panic attack he had while traveling for research, which he eventually escaped by observing some birds in the forest, I think. Anyway, he uses it to point out that as humans much of our anxiety often stems from the powerful symbolic nature of language, and how the plasticity of language can allow our conceptualizations to spiral quite far beyond what might actually be happening in our shared physical world. And we can become momentarily lost in that rift. But by placing ourselves amongst a variety of other multi-species languages and behavioral logics, we're able to once again bridge that gap and find alternative routes back to a shared, grounded environment. So in a sense I think that's what watching animal behavior does—it reminds us unconsciously of alternative ways of thinking, being, rooting, and existing, which allow us to escape the potential precipices within our own mind.

F: Wow, yes, yes, that's absolutely fantastic. You're actually the second person to recommend that now, so I must be sure to write it down.

L: It's interesting to think about how plants and animals are discovering their own alternative uses for human cultural artifacts, and how this might be facilitating the evolution of new niches or species within urban ecosystems. But I wonder if another benefit of welcoming nonhuman species to our cities is that, through their alternative spatial logics and disruptive antagonisms, they might be putting a productive selective pressure on our own creative evolution, and contributing to our ability to find inspiration regarding our own adaptive potential.

F: Yes, I see what you're saying. With the macaques, you see, it's tricky. There's really two sides to the coin. They are much more mischievous than the langurs, who simply eat the leaves of the city's trees more or less. Langurs get fed at certain rooftops and temples, so their food security in general is quite high. Whereas macaques, they are doing daily raids on

fig. 6
Ravi is the narcissistic one.
(Photo: Donald M. Broom)

the food markets to get their required amount of food. They're also given food at the temples, but it is often much less clear when they're going to get it. And so they have to be quite clever in their stealing—they must watch and understand human behavior in order to grab something when someone's back is turned or they're distracted. While we never managed to film it, our guide said that they actually tend to steal from young women more than anyone else, as if they've learned from humans to target what they see as more vulnerable.

So while the langurs don't have a confusing time with humans, the macaques often have a very confusing time. The langurs are rarely mistreated, but the macaques are under constant attack. They'll have water buckets thrown on them or they'll be beaten with sticks. And yet, literally the next hour that stall owner might end up feeding those same macaques. It's very strange. Perhaps it depends on the cycles of the market—who's there and what buyers want at a certain time. But it must be very difficult for the macaques to tune into these cycles, and to know when they're approaching the food market whether they'll be welcomed or scared away.

But, to compare, do you know about the funerals that happen in langur society? If a langur is found dead, often from electrocution when they hold two powerlines and close the circuit—and especially if it's on a Tuesday, which is Hanuman day—then they will be given a full funeral. The monkey will be taken to the temple, and a throne will be built and garland set around it, and the langur will be painted with *bindi* and all kinds of bright paint. It'll be carried on the throne through the streets and that procession will take two to three hours, and people will join along as it moves, gathering and playing music. At the end it will receive a traditional human funeral. They'll cremate it and so on. And it's just extraordinary that that many people will take that much time out of their

I truly believe that one of the most powerful ways we can create support for the care of animals in our cities is through architectural design of shared habitats.

day to participate if they come across a procession of the dead langur. I think that shows the real intensity of how they are revered and where they sit in the cultural imagination. And I think that's quite far from our respect for animals in the Western world. It's hard to imagine a kind of mass outpouring of love in the way there is for lots of animals in Indian cities. In the West, our care is more predicated on the practice of people of sufficient power working to protect certain animals, which are often prized for aesthetic reasons as we discussed. Either that, or it becomes a question of economics, in which case we might try to quantify a species' ecological benefits or contributions to our mental health.

But I truly believe that one of the most powerful ways we can create support for the care of animals in our cities is through the architectural design or allowance of shared habitats. The fact that in Jodhpur you're constantly seeing langurs jump six meters right before you, this phenomenal parkour, is amazing. In Britain we love our bird feeders, you know, and we try to stop the squirrels from getting at it. But in reality, we get so much entertainment from watching their cheeky little attempts to get past all the little hurdles and get at the seeds. So I think there are ways to design animal habitats that are hospitable and ecologically sound but also transparent and entertaining. Have you seen the buildings with bird boxes integrated into the walls? I love that. At my house we have these little "mini beast hotels" for insects and bees, and the kids just love watching these things. I think there's lots of fun to be had in thinking through how to create these dramas and spectacles, which as we've already discussed, have truly deep and profound impacts. So I truly love the approach to your journal, you know. Mischief and such. There is much to be said for searching for opportunities for light and delight in the context of very daunting design challenges. I think it is essential. 🐇

Scheduling Pleasure

Kyle J Gename

> "So—the way one should answer the conservative platitude according to which every honest man has a profound need to believe in something is to say that every honest man has a profound need to find another subject who will believe in his place."
>
> – Slavoj Žižek[1]

1
Slavoj Žižek, *The Plague of Fantasies*. (London: Verso, 1997).

My jeans felt heavy on my legs so I couldn't help but remain perfectly still. I was lying flat on my back, not having moved since I went down. My eyelids cranked open over eyes that were still asleep. I exited the bed to confirm I had everything on my final checklist. Everything was there, but I felt like I was forgetting something. I sat on the edge of the bed, staring at my bulging panniers, entertaining the idea that someone else could bike this weekend. My stomach churned and constricted with a mixture of guilt, trepidation, and processed foods. The hardest thing to do, after all, is start.

Even so, I checked the weather report for each of my overnight stops, scrolled through my Facebook timeline, and texted my friend, brother-in-law, and housemate that I had started my ride. *OMG good luck!* It would be foolish not to go at this point. I bound myself to begin by saying that I already had. *Be safe and text me when you stop for dinner.* By that point, I realized I was hungry, and it would be unwise to begin in that condition. *All Things Considered* hummed from my phone while I inserted a PB&J. *Should I download an audiobook for the ride? No. I'll probably miss an important turn.* My arsenal of stalling techniques was running low. After an hour or so of dawdling, I was out the door (albeit hopelessly behind schedule and already dreading the idea of making my way south well after dusk).

That September I decided to give up *Give up? No, it will be so worth it!* my Thanksgiving break to bike from Charlottesville to Durham and surprise my sister for dinner. I don't have a car, so my sister chauffeurs me on holidays. This year was different. *Oh Candace, don't worry about Thanksgiving this year, I'm riding down with a friend.* It was fun to tell a white lie; my Fuji Traverse was a friend, after all.

The multi-state bike tour plot burgeoned into a fantasy. I would disconnect from a burdensome stream of duty fulfillment and dissociate myself from the everyday drudgery of school and work. This long-distance ride would outweigh the sober and sterile studio hours I was racking up. *That's what a break is for, honey.* I wanted to feel the wind on my face and solicit a mental blankness that I had not allowed in a long time. I was pleased to relieve my chauffeur sister this go-round but was also driven by a visceral desire to move. *Listen to your body.*

The trip would also produce ideal content for my Insta. I'm quite selective in what I post *Practice your curatorial skills* but don't get the chance to travel often. I knew most other students would be out of town for break and at least a few would be going someplace cool or historic. I didn't want to miss out on engaging my followers. I remained vigilant for any Instagram-worthy views.

I felt satisfied with my progress a few hours after leaving Charlottesville. I smiled realizing I was not turning around; I would keep riding south even if I didn't make it all the way to Durham. I stopped for water, to update my directions, and to begin photo documentation. *You haven't posted in a while, what's on your mind?* The bodily memories of straining my quads to mount hills or bobbling in the saddle over loose gravel have a higher resolution than these images. As the sky began to flush, I was haunted by my late start. A phantasmic load compounded on the bike's panniers as I pedaled, thighs searing. There was no chance that I would make it to Lynchburg before complete darkness overtook the path.

The following two days and 200 miles continued in much the same way: overly meticulous late-night route mapping, oversleeping, consenting to the flows of dread, and ten to twelve hours of firing on all cylinders to make up for lost time. A metronomic mental count *1-2-3-4-5-6-7-8* registered each pedal forward. I took a limited number of pictures, lest I lose even more time dilly-dallying on some overlook. *All's well that ends well, eh?* I only stopped for food or water, precluding some idyllic shots from the virtual newsfeed. *The punchline's what you're after, then.* Thursday morning I rehearsed the blow-by-blow I would give my family over the Thanksgiving table. The optics of my bike tour were very good. *You rode how far?* In truth, I had been crafting the story for weeks. *What a beast!* Although I was constantly busy with school and work, I still had enough time to devote to exercise and long distance training. *He's so well-rounded!* I could recount the story of the headless doe I found on the shoulder or the numerous close calls with automobile traffic to maintain their interest. *This is why I worry about you!*

I was nearly late for dinner that evening and, had it not been for a series of Virginia state troopers turning a blind eye to my frenetic pedaling down I-29 S, I probably would have had to call the trip early and concede defeat. *It ain't about the journey.* But come the eleventh hour, I was streaming down my sister's cul-de-sac, composing the final details of the tale.

Sitting at the dinner table, however, I felt neither proud nor satisfied. The joke about my sore perineum I suppose wasn't for mixed company. *You must be tired dear.* I waited for a sense of enlightenment or accomplishment to develop. It didn't. In its absence, I felt a wave of regret. Regret that I hadn't enjoyed myself along the way, or that my trip had been a chance to aggrandize myself. Had I relinquished opportunities for actual enjoyment to my social media account? Had I just devoted three days for "unplugging" only to end up giving away the trip to my followers?

———

There is a psychoanalytical term for this kind of behavior, something Robert Pfaller refers to as "interpassivity." In *The Aesthetics of Delegated Enjoyment*, Pfaller reveals these impulses as a paradoxical condition of the modern world, explaining that, "whereas interactivity entails shifting a part of the artistic production ('activity') from the artwork to the viewer, here the opposite occurs: the viewing ('passivity') is shifted from the viewer to the artwork."[2] Interpassivity thus involves a transference of enjoyment from subject to external object. Pfaller and Slovenian philosopher Slavoj Žižek offer the example of a VCR, which "enjoys" the recorded program in the place of the busy person who hits "record" on their way out the door. According to Pfaller & Žižek, the subject relinquishes its control to the fetish object, allowing it to enjoy on the subject's behalf. These fetish objects, like VCRs and social media posts, can even preempt and shape our enjoyment, dictating when and how we should enjoy. This type of prescribed enjoyment is found in the commentary of Greek choruses and through the laugh tracks of countless '90s sitcoms. Žižek asks, "Do we not witness 'interpassivity' in a great number of today's publicity spots or posters which, as it were, passively enjoy the product instead of us? (Coke cans containing the inscription 'Ooh! Ooh! What a taste!' emulate the ideal customer's reaction in advance.)"[3]

Žižek warns that rapid developments in technology, especially vis-à-vis the formation of cyberspace, have elevated the potential risks of interpassivity: "the paradox is that with the spectralization of the fetish, with the progressive disintegration of its positive materiality, its presence becomes even more oppressive and all-pervasive, as if there is no way the subject can escape its hold."[2] For Žižek, invisible fetish objects (how does Google know what I want to buy?) become omnipotent over the subject, radically altering the status of our subjectivity. Facebook, that ubiquitous

2
Robert Pfaller, *Interpassivity: The Aesthetics of Delegated Enjoyment* (Edinburgh: Edinburgh University Press, 2017).

3
Slavoj Žižek, *The Plague of Fantasies*. (London: Verso, 1997).

and clandestine social media behemoth, prompts us to enjoy, but also to share, post, and message through disembodied taglines.

Social media is both immediate and public. Understood in this way, sharing enjoyable goings-on via social media has transformed from something carefree into something of a societal obligation. In order to fulfill my duty to "take it all in," I curated my trip through Instagram. With every post, my feed lit up with red hearts, and my role as active participant was subsumed by a passive medium (my phone) which proceeded to "like" the experience for me.

Is it possible, however, that I posted photos to relieve myself of the obligation to engage? Although I took the pictures absentmindedly at the time, might I have done it knowing that I would engage with them later? Žižek is highly skeptical of these possibilities: "Is not 'to be relieved of one's enjoyment' a meaningless paradox, at best a euphemism for simply being deprived of it? Is enjoyment not something which, precisely, cannot be done through the Other? … the so-called threat of the new media lies in the fact that they deprive us of our passivity, or our authentic passive experience, and thus prepare us for mindless frenetic activity."[4]

The popularity of movies like *Her* and series like *Black Mirror* reflect (and perhaps overstate) society's fear and fascination with social media entanglements and the subordination of human agency. Some narratives conclude that to find real pleasure and enjoyment, we must strive to remain active participants. However, these productions are as reductive as they are sensational. They conflate the emergence of powerful techno-fetish objects like Instagram with a carefully engineered conspiracy to alter human subjectivity. As a society, we acknowledge the impotence of social media apps like Instagram to keep people connected—ask a millennial about the hollow significance of becoming "Facebook official." Why, then, if Facebook is unable to fulfill its intended function, are we so frightened by interpassivity?

Simply put: because it's possible. Although Žižek is a major whistleblower against interpassivity, he acknowledges that, under certain circumstances, "by surrendering my innermost content, including my dreams and anxieties, to the Other, a space opens up in which I am free to breathe: when the Other laughs for me, I am free to take a rest; when the Other is sacrificed instead of me, I am free to go on living with the awareness that I did atone for my guilt; and so on."[5]

Although I used Instagram to enjoy in my place, I still had fun between these actions of passivity. There were times when I found both active and passive pleasure simultaneously. Furthermore, choosing to be passive was an action unto itself, and should not be misinterpreted as an absence of action. Instagram took one for the team, or rather, I made Insta take the burden, thus freeing me to enjoy in parallel and in private.

Gijs Van Oenen points out that "interpassive behavior signals a kind of wariness, and even resistance, regarding the demands of interactive life. The interpassive subject desperately wants to remain 'loyal', or true, to the interactive relation, yet indicates a desire to be released from its

4
Slavoj Žižek, "The Interpassive Subject," *Centre Georges Pompidou*, 1998, accessed March 1 2017, http://www.lacan.com/zizek-pompidou.html.

5
Ibid.

burden … we may also view interpassivity, on the other hand, as a form of resistance against the conglomerate of interactive systems—whether we identify this as modernity, emancipation, capitalism, or disciplinary society, to name but a few."[6]

Social media, this newly powerful "Other" teaches us, guides us, delays us, enjoys for and with us, but that should not induce some widespread existential crisis for humanity. Our motivations, our desires, and our pleasures can be reflected upon and revised. People have lived vicariously through one another, for better or for worse, for a long time. 🐰

6

Gijs van Oenen, "Interpassivity revisited: a critical and historical reappraisal of interpassive phenomena." *International Journal of Žižek Studies* 2, no. 2 (2016).

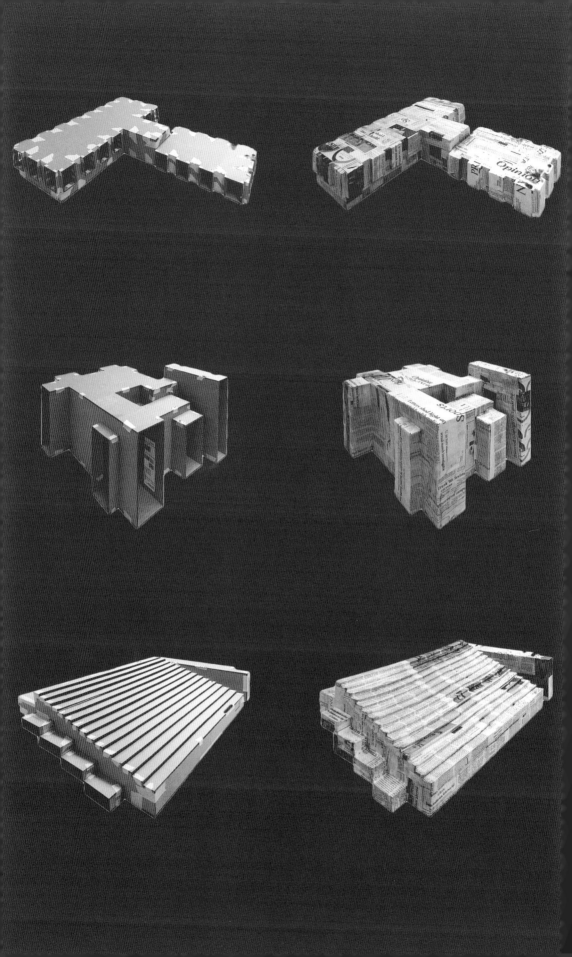

The Piñata: A Treatise

Ryan Roark, Laura Salazar, and Weiwei Zhang

These are piñatas of models of buildings.

Traditionally, a piñata is a scaled and abstracted figure of a real object—often an animal—that is filled with objects, suspended, and broken open by blindfolded contenders during a celebration. A piñata may look like a donkey; but because of the abstraction, scaling, suspension from normal context, and celebration, the piñata is not a stand-in for the donkey. When children hit the piñata to break it, they are simply trying to reach its contents, rather than performing an act of violence against the donkey.

The practice of architecture involves translation between buildings and drawings, as well as between buildings and models. Multiple iterations across different media allow for productive interpretations that can produce new forms, new spaces, or new relationships.[1] The establishment of a new representational object into this chain, previously foreign to architecture, creates new renditions and draws attention to the strangeness of the discipline's conventions that we may otherwise take for granted. Unlike a model, a piñata has function beyond representation, and brings an element of performance and unpredictability into the representational cycle.

The move from model to piñata is akin to the move from building to model.[2] The transition from a building to a model or a drawing is always a move towards abstraction, which includes selective removal of large amounts of detail and content. The evolution from a model to a piñata

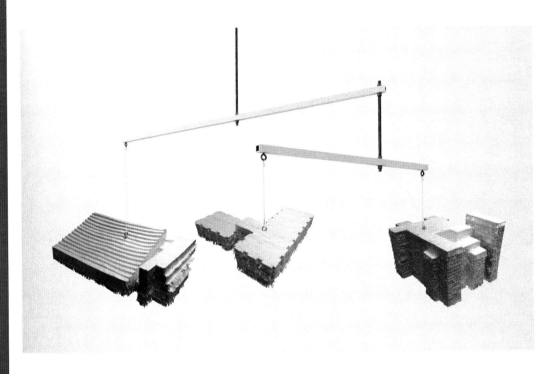

involves creating a functional object with specific materiality, and is therefore a move towards realism. The piñata is not lacking in any detail; it is full-scale and fully functional. At the same time, with respect to the building, the move from model to piñata is a further abstraction that creates new reading.[3] Without this move, for instance, we might not think to put fringe on a building, to fill a building with candy and streamers, or to crack open a building's façade.[4]

The introduction of the new piñata medium highlights assumptions we make about other media with which we are already too comfortable. It is certainly unusual to see an object that represents a building hanging in mid-air at a 45-degree angle with neither ground nor context, but many of us don't bat an eye at a siteless worm's-eye axonometric drawing.[5] The knowledge that the most exciting part of the piñata is contained inside indicates the strangeness of a sculptural (non-sectional) approach to model-making. The method of piñata construction adds several more layers of strangeness: for instance, the papier-mâché process is the application of a continuous surface across multiple members and joints.

The buildings selected for translation to the piñata medium by way of models should be architectural primitives, considering this project addresses foundational questions of materiality, structure, and architectural representation standards.[vi] A Renaissance piñata project might take Palladian villas as its subject matter, while a mid-twentieth-century piñata project would likely look to Le Corbusier and Mies van der Rohe. Today, however, a fundamental manifestation of architectural zeitgeist does not present itself. The use of architectural education institutions underscores the lack of a formal center for the discipline in the twenty-first century, and proposes that the institutions themselves are the most stable center in modern day.

fig. 2 (previous spread)
Princeton's School of Architecture building, piñata-tized.

fig. 3 (above)
Piñata mobile of the Harvard Graduate School of Design, the Princeton School of Architecture, and the Yale School of Architecture (Photo: Ryan Roark)

Finally, it should be noted that these piñatas are in unstable equilibrium with each other by a visible relational system and by the weight of contents that are not visible until the exterior is cracked open.[7] This assembly is intended to heighten the anticipation of revealing and releasing the contents, as well as to suggest the nature of the relationship between different representational media. When this piñata mobile is hit with an external force, the components are destabilized and require time to reach equilibrium once again.[8] The movement is erratic, and perhaps even a bit dangerous. At the very least, it momentarily alleviates boredom.[9] 🐇

Endnotes

(1) Harold Bloom identifies six different ways in which poets achieve misreading or "misprision" of their predecessors, in order to escape the "anxiety of influence" and produce new work. Perhaps most analogous to the creation of piñata from building model is kenosis: "a breaking-device similar to the defense mechanisms our psyches employ against repetition compulsions; kenosis then is a movement towards discontinuity with the precursor. I take the word from St. Paul, where it means the humbling or emptying out of Jesus by himself, when he accepts reduction from divine to human status. The later poet, apparently emptying himself of his own afflatus, his imaginative godhood, seems to humble himself as though he were ceasing to be a poet, but this ebbing is so performed in relation to a precursor's poem-of-ebbing that the precursor is emptied out also, and so the later poem of deflation is not as absolute as it seems" (*The Anxiety of Influence: A Theory of Poetry*, Oxford: Oxford University Press, 1997, p. 14-15). The emptying-out by the breaking device of the piñata produces, if not new poetry, then certainly great happiness.

(2) In "Translations from Drawing to Building" (1986), Robin Evans compares the processes of translation that occur between media in architecture to those between different languages, pointing out that translations will inevitably change the content to some extent in the process. He writes, "I would like to suggest that something similar occurs in architecture between the [piñata] and the building, and that a similar suspension of critical disbelief is necessary in order to enable architects to perform their task at all. I would like to suggest also that, while such an enabling fiction may be made explicit, this has not been done in architecture, and that because of this inexplicitness a curious situation has come to pass in which, while on the one hand the [piñata] might be vastly overvalued, on the other the properties of [piñata]—its peculiar powers in relation to its putative subject, the building—are hardly recognized at all. Recognition of the [piñata's] power as a medium turns out, unexpectedly, to be recognition of the [piñata's] distinctness from and unlikeness to the thing that is represented, rather than its likeness to it, which is neither as paradoxical nor as dissociative as it may seem" (*Translations from Drawings to Buildings and Other Essays*, London: Architectural Association, 1997, p. 154).

(3) A possibly not-inconsequential close aesthetic relative of these piñatas is Hirsuta's project Raspberry Fields, a house with curled shingles,

which, like the fringe on the piñata, begin relatively flat and uniform but are detached and curled as they age. As Jason Payne explained in his exhibition opening for "Rawhide: the New Shingle Style" at SCI-Arc in 2011, these formal explorations came about thanks to extradisciplinary explorations, in this case into hairstyling (SCI-Arc Media Archive, July 29, 2011). It is hoped that explorations into piñata-making (and breaking) may catalyze similarly interdisciplinary synthetic operations.

(4) The relationship of ornament to architecture has become complicated in the past century. Adolf Loos is perhaps the most prominent protestor of decoration thanks to his essay "Ornament and Crime" (1929). Loos objects to ornament on both aesthetic and moral grounds: "Ornament means wasted labor and therefore wasted health. That was always the case. Today, however, it also means wasted material, and both mean wasted capital" (*Ornament and Crime: Selected Essays*, Riverside, CA: Ariadne Press, 1998, p. 171). However, it should be noted that in the case of a piñata, the ornament (fringe) is in fact a great conservator of time, energy, and perfection, as it can be used to mitigate and distract from almost any defect in construction. In fact, there is ample reason to believe Adolf Loos makes an exception to his rule for the piñata, as he writes: "The form of an object should last, that is, we should find it tolerable as long as the object itself lasts." A piñata, then, is not unaesthetic as it is only required to be tolerable for the length of a three-year-old's birthday party—usually not a particularly drawn-out affair.

(5) Similarities between these piñatas as hung and Peter Eisenman's drawings of House II have not gone unnoticed, with the one obvious difference that House II is not full of hidden candy.

(6) The concept of reappropiating building forms as primitive building blocks for new forms of representation or even for new buildings is not a new concept. It was integral, for instance, to the Beaux-Arts approach to the ancients, or to Nicholas Hawksmoor's creation of his six London churches. Historian Kerry Downes has cited Hawksmoor's use of pyramids, temple fronts, and other apparently historic references as examples of geometric purity instead of historicism: "[H]e took literally and developed what his masters claimed only with a great deal of salt: geometry as the basis of architecture ... By thinking of architecture in terms of solid geometry he made of style a kind of costume which could be Roman, Greek ... or even Gothic" (Hawksmoor: an exhibition of models, drawings and recent photographs, organised in conjunction with the Hawksmoor Committee's campaign for preserving Christ Church, Spitalfields, and St. Anne's, Limehouse, Arts Council of Great Britain, 1962, p. 8). From the piñata's point of view, any building or animal will do for a shape, as the piñata does not read cultural meaning into shape.

(7) The piñata of Harvard GSD's Gund Hall holds more candy than the piñatas of Princeton SoA and Yale SoA combined, weighing in at over 20 pounds. The Harvard piñata is also the hardest to break, as the stepped "trays" prove highly structural in piñata form. The Princeton piñata cracks open with just one or two swift swings of the bat, thanks to its L-shaped plan.

(8) Equilibrium calculations have been rigorously carried out based on

a casual perusal of Daniel Schodek's *Structures* (Seventh Edition) and slides from Sigrid Adriaenssens's lecture "Equilibrium" from ARC 510, "Structural Analysis for Architecture" (September 2014). Additionally, the teaching assistant for this course has confirmed that, assuming fixed joints, zero friction, and no force to the cross-members, this mobile will not fall down.

(9) Any important architecture project takes seriously both site and program. The syllabus for ARC 501 describes the Site/Program of this project as follows: "Imagine that the mobile is an instrument for ameliorating or mediating boredom" (Michael Meredith, 2014).

Three Days in the Desert

Dominique van Olm

What follows is a photo essay with editorial détournement *in the form of quotes from Jean Baudrillard's* America, 1988.

"Geological—and hence metaphysical—monumentality, by contrast with the physical altitude of ordinary landscapes. Upturned relief patterns, sculpted out by wind, water, and ice, dragging you down into the whirlpool of time, into the remorseless eternity of a slow-motion catastrophe."

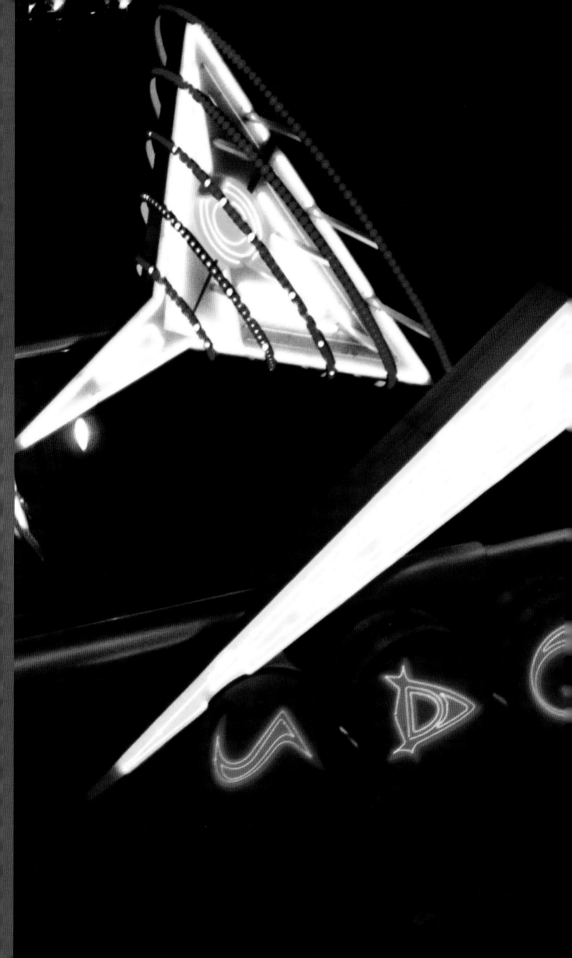

"The inhumanity of our ulterior, asocial, superficial world immediately finds its aesthetic form here, its ecstatic form. For the desert is simply that: an ecstatic critique of culture, an ecstatic form of disappearance."

"There is a sort of miracle in the insipidity of artificial paradises, so
long as they achieve the greatness of an entire (un)culture. In America,
space lends a sense of grandeur even to the insipidity of the suburbs and
'funky towns.' The desert is everywhere, preserving insignificance."

"All that is cold and dead in desertification or social enucleation rediscovers its contemplative form here in the heat of the desert. Here in the transversality of the desert and the irony of geology, the transpolitical finds its generic, mental space."

"The Italian miracle: that of stage and scene.
The American miracle: that of the obscene.
The profusion of sense, as against the deserts of meaninglessness."

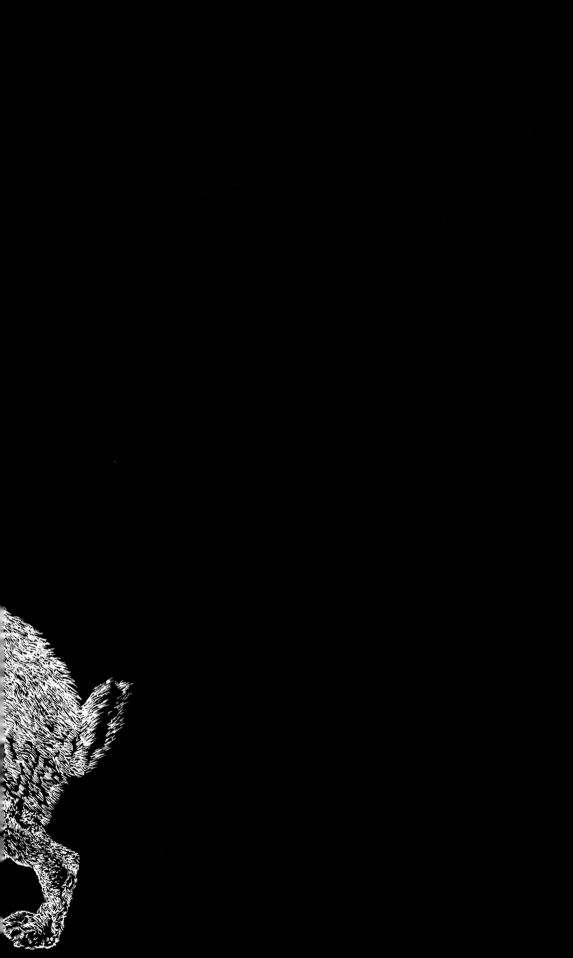

OKAY, NOW:

Rip up this page and throw it in the air.

"Quiet Riot": A Conversation with Ross Exo Adams

The Editors

Sarah (L1): So we have a list of lightning round questions that we like to start with. Really quick, you don't have to think too hard about them.

Ross (R): *[inaudible]* … put me on the spot…

L1: Yeah, no, they're very quick. Number one: what's in your pockets?

R: Nothing!

Maddie (L2): Nothing at all?

R: Nothing. Well, fuzz probably? But other than that, nothing.

L1: Okay.

L2: Okay, number two: what's the last thing you threw away?

[long pause, laughter]

R: I have no idea. I have no idea. Probably some piece of paper that my son left on the floor or something. Detritus of my child.

L2: Gotcha.

L1: Okay, number three: favorite band in high school?

R: *[pause]* Quiet Riot.

L1 + 2: Hmm.

L1: I don't know what that is.

R: I'm being mischievous.

[laughter]

R: You said to answer quickly.

L2: Answer quickly. First thing that comes to mind even if it's completely factually inaccurate. Um. What's your zodiac sign?

R: Gemini.

L1: Number five: what did you want to be when you were growing up?

R: A doctor! And ironically, I became one, but not the kind my mom probably wanted me to be.

L2 (to L1): Does this apply?

L1 (to L2): Yeah.

L2: Okay, what would you want to be if you couldn't be an architect?

R: An academic?

L2: No, you can't have that one either.

R: Okay, okay, um… what would I want to be…

L2: Is it "doctor"?

R: A ski instructor? That's kind of a lame answer but we'll go with it.

L2: First thing that comes to mind.

L1: Number seven: favorite tree?

R: How's it called… a gingko?

L1: You know, that's a common answer. Interesting. *[pause]* I'm not trying to make you feel bad.

L2: Number eight: largest animal you've killed?

fig. 1 (above)
Some options for "largest animal ever killed."
(Image: The British Library)

R: Perhaps a deer.

L2: Perhaps?

R: But I'm not sure.

L1: Number nine: guilty pleasure?

R: Guilty pleasure? Uh, it's gonna be something lame like Netflix or something.

[laughter]

R: I dunno, long showers? That's also lame. That's so lame. Does this get published, by the way?

L1: We don't know. We're not sure.

L2: We'll see.

L1: We're not sure what the point of these questions is.

L2: Um, okay, number ten: cats vs. dogs?

R: Uh, dogs.

L2: Okay, the interview is over.

[laughter]

L2: We're cat people.

R: You know, I have two friends from UVA who are "Extreme Cat People" who are teaching with me now so… there's something going on there in Charlottesville, I don't know what.

L2: Yeah, I dunno.

L1: I feel like there are a lot of dog people here.

L2: I feel like Charlottesville's a dog town.

R: That makes sense to me.

L2: Like, "wholesomeness" and "dogs."

R: Golden retrievers everywhere. *[pause]* Totally.

L2: Um, okay, thank you for that informative lightning round. You got our questions that we emailed to you?

L1: Maybe we should start … we were gonna talk a little bit about why we chose "mischief."

R: Yeah, I was about to ask you that actually.

L1: We kind of went into it in one of the questions but I think, to give some context, we feel like as students there's this narrative or just … I don't know what you'd call it—

L2: Ideology?

L1: Ideology … something in school that is very crisis-oriented and problem solving-oriented, fixing things [and so on]. There's a pressure to kind of solve the world's problems … and the world's problems are very large … and concerning.

L2: *[laughing]* "Concerning."

L1: They're concerning. It's concerning. So I feel that we were interested in mischief because it is not—

L2: "Productive."

L1: Productive, necessarily; it's not about optimizing, it's not about clear solutions.

L2: It's counterproductive, sometimes. But sometimes just … uh …

R: Yeah, it's productive in other ways and transforms the problem itself, in a way.

L1: Yeah, so I think it came a little bit out of a frustration with the rhetoric of school.

L2: "The discourse."

L1: The design discourse.

R: "The discourse."

[laughter]

L1: Um, so yeah, I feel like a lot of your work speaks about that rhetoric [of crisis] so maybe you could just talk a little bit about that and your thoughts on it.

R: Absolutely. I think it's the number-one downfall of architectural discourse at the moment—that confronted with the problems that we face, we feel that the only way to approach it is through this kind of basic commandeering of modernism, of "functionality" that now transforms itself into solutionism and so forth. And it's really deprived architecture from so many points of view; on the one hand its capacity to imagine worlds and imagine different worlds—that are fundamentally different from the world that we are forced to inhabit. It goes beyond architecture, this is not just a school thing, this is everywhere. It's a meta-discursive tendency right now. This moment of perpetual crisis also deprives us of the capacity of history to speak to us in the present, and therefore to think about what the future might mean. And I don't want to think about "the future" in the sort of modernist sense where we are all moving toward this kind of destiny of techno-utopia, or whatever, but rather as thinking of different worlds that are better for people. Certain people, maybe, or at least—better within a strategic agenda. Technological solutionism pretends to be a project that's better for everyone, while at the same time not imagining new futures, not imagining a different world, imagining a world whose cracks are kind of technologically sutured together so as to keep the world we have from falling apart … which, it seems to be falling apart.

We do that in part because we've transformed history from something that vibrantly lives on in the present—as somebody like Walter Benjamin might say—into a set of a data and a set of precedents that then project into the present as ready-made scenarios and ways of "future-proofing" and so forth. I feel like it's a really sad time in many ways but also really exciting for that same reason. There's so much to do for architects and, uh, the tools at present don't give us the opportunity.

L2: I feel like—well we've been reading your work—I was wondering if you could talk specifically about landscape [architecture] and how it's sort of vulnerable to this kind of techno-utopianism. Maybe uniquely so, maybe even more than architecture in a certain way.

R: Yeah, totally. I mean at this point—I'm probably late in saying this but architecture has somewhat discredited itself because of like the late '90s, early 2000s height of "star-chitecture" or whatever, Dubai and so on— and I think that there's a lot of justified blowback to that. Something

like landscape architecture has been framed as a counterpoint to more object-centered modes of practice, in ways that can be illuminating but also reductive. I should say that I'm not an expert on landscape at all; my main research is into certain projects today; for example, "Rebuild by Design" and others but also the history of landscape, and that's maybe where I have a little bit more of a grasp.

When we see landscape as this surface of provision, this set of stages, stages where "processes" are enacted, this set of ephemeral phases, all these things that James Corner spoke about a while ago, we treat it as a sort of trans-historical category, equivalent to "the earth" or "ground" or "geology"—but even geology is of course historically situated. And I think that when we do that, we miss a lot of deeply, deeply political connections that landscape has historically had with the construction of the State, with the construction of Western or Euro-centric forms of power that have sort of exported themselves and generalized themselves into the sort of State construction that we now have today. When we treat landscape as this "set of processes" and "nature" and so forth, we don't see that our actions in the present reconstruct new political technologies in the effort to deal with the problems that previous regimes have caused.

Again, the "Rebuild by Design" project is something I'm looking at because of the deployment of all sorts of cybernetic and so-called "nature-based solutions" that, you know, attempt to sort of monitor and collect massive amounts of data, not only about people in the city but also about ecologies and the relationship between the two. I'm quite skeptical of that because it's not that it just suggests a sort of tie with new forms of governmentality but it speaks about it directly: there's this attempt to create a sort of seamless, scaleless form of management that's written into new laws and forms of controlling the population, movements in cities, and so forth—all in the name of, you know, "emergency" and "crisis-management" but of course with much more insidious implications.

L1: Is that the OMA project? The "Rebuild by Design" … or is that something different?

R: Yeah, they're part of it, I think there's ten teams. They're all working around the greater New York City area, so it's also a scaling-up of design—treating a regional-scale design as something accessible to architectural knowledge. Which is interesting.

L2: It's sort of like "ecology" has morphed into an ideology, like what you're saying about how science presents itself as objective and no one can—who can argue with science? And then on top of it there's the narrative—that I think is good in some ways but in other ways kind of toxic—is the "Well, we are nature," and so if we are nature, and if ecology can constantly be monitored and controlled, then the implication is that we can also constantly be monitored and controlled. I think you've written a lot about that, if you want to talk a little bit about the body as [a site of surveillance and control].

R: Yeah, it's a project that I'm just beginning and it's difficult when you start teaching to do research like I once did when I was a Ph.D. student, but it's something that I'm thinking a lot about. I'm trying to collect ways in which we represent the body—not only represent but also project as a sort of common piece of knowledge this idea of "the body." How do we understand the body collectively, what ways are we constructing to perceive the body? I think one of the becoming-dominant modes of representation is to see the body as not separate and individuated and outside of nature but part of nature, open to it, and kind of an ecology itself. A body has other bodies in it—bacteria, things that we breathe in—so we also collapse notions like ecology and ecosystems across scales. I am an ecosystem, my arm is an ecosystem, you know—everything about me—and I sit within a larger ecosystem and that sits within a larger ecosystem. There's this issue of scalelessness that I find fascinating, but aside from that, we are constructing this notion of an infinitely open body. But when we do that, because we have the technological capacity to monitor and measure various parts of those ecosystems, we're also opening ourselves up to increasing monitoring—increasing forms of control. It's not a coercive form of control necessarily, but through information circulation and so on, we control ourselves, effectively.

It's something I've been thinking a lot about, I don't have a clear answer to that, I've been talking about it as humans "becoming infrastructural," which I think separates or makes distinct our previously "modern" relationship to infrastructure where infrastructures were about managing bodies and so they were constructed to be understood in a kind of corporeal sense through our movements in the city and we responded to infrastructure. Now I think it's becoming part of us. We no longer see it in a way. There's a lot of danger in that, just as much as there are benefits to being able to understand ourselves and understand our impact in the world and all that stuff.

L2: Is there some kind of remedy to this, do you feel?

R: A "solution"? Yes, I have the answer!

L1: Well, I'm curious if you've seen other approaches.

L2: Or, I guess to add onto that in a way, do you think maybe there is a danger of some kind of neo-romanticism that is in itself reactionary? You know, like, oh now we have to go back and repeat all the mistakes of individualism.

R: Well, I'm not sure what you mean about repeating all the mistakes of individualism.

L2: Well, just this idea that ecology is "opening the body" or opening things up—and that has a certain effect—but then I feel like the reactionary mode would be to try to reclaim "the soul."

R: I mean, there is that. Again, the different ontologies that are emerging, and have been for a while, the human / non-human / more-than-human—all of these are very useful and this is not to reject them categorically. I think, in terms of like, "what to do" in a way … because like you say there is a potential reactionary tendency, not to mention the romanticism of like "Let's make the body great again!" You ask if there are models out there to intervene in this sort of techno-utopic, quasi-scientific solutionism … I'm working to try to do that myself. I think there's a lot of interesting models out there that don't necessarily come from architecture.

1
Not An Alternative is a NY-based collective and non-profit organization that works at the intersection of art, activism, and pedagogy. See http://notanalternative.org/.

In architecture we tend to get into things late, so artists might be working on really interesting problems that architects then pick up on ten years later. I've worked with a group of people called Not An Alternative[1] and they do really interesting art-activist work, specifically around the space of the museum and the natural history museum. Their concern has to do with things like climate change and the museum of natural history as a site of knowledge-production and truth-telling, how it narrates or erases certain aspects of climate change, how it turns it into diagrammatic processes that happen and you learn about them and go home and you recycle a bit more and maybe get some chickens or something like that.

And that's the problem. And here we come back to individuality; the response we're taught to have is to privatize the concept of climate change. Even things like "resilience": I remember there was a statement for 100 Resilient Cities sponsored by the Rockefeller Foundation, they had this slogan, "Resilience starts with you." It's this idea that climate change is based on the cumulative effect of humans and so the solution is that we need to behave better. This is the so-called "nudge theory." And I think that's an extremely dangerous proposition because of course it strips the extremely political and historical formation of climate change in the first place from the actual phenomenon of climate change.

> *This moment of perpetual crisis deprives us of the capacity of history to speak to us in the present, and therefore to think about what the future might mean.*

But in the same way that I can maybe recycle more and have chickens or something, I cannot access capitalism. I cannot transform capitalism myself. I cannot even think about the problem of capitalism being central to the effects of climate change because it's my fault that climate change is happening, and it's your fault, and it's everyone's fault collectively. We've turned it into this privatized, moralized issue, and I think—coming back to the group Not An Alternative—what they're proposing is rather to use the power of an institution like a museum of natural history—to use its institutional space, its capital, its cultural capital, as a site of contestation. By inhabiting the role of a museum—they've gotten a certification, they call themselves The Natural History Museum—they've been able to access conferences and be invited to enter into the networks of power of natural history museums around the world, so they're actually able to create discussions and debates with the people involved in natural history museums and to actually foment resistance from within. And they've had really great effects, they've gotten one of the Koch brothers kicked off the board of the Smithsonian and other really substantial victories that we couldn't do on our own or through more traditional forms of activism.

I'm personally interested in that kind of thing and when I try to think about that as a "design strategy," what's important is not to think about climate change as a problem to solve: we can't. We can build sustainable buildings and all that stuff but that's not changing the whole story. What we need is to recover—and to remember let's say—the politics and to make visible the networks of power that make climate change what it is. So it's something that I'm trying to think about through creating alternative forms of museums of natural history or alternative histories of nature. It's a lot of fun, actually, and it does seem to coincide with the notion of "mischief" to a degree, but I think it's also something that has a lot of—I don't know so much about mischief, historically, as a category of thought—but I feel like the goal of mischief is mischief itself. I would, I would suspect that. And I think that what we're trying to do is inhabit modes of mischief-making with an ambition to achieve something beyond disruption. If design is to be relevant in the realm of climate change, yes, ecology is fine and we need windmills and solar panels and all that but we also need to find new ways to create publics, to create discourse, to create "discord." To disrupt the smooth flow of capital, to disrupt the networks that make the world seem infinitely available to continue capitalist expansion of networks and circulation.

L1: Do you think that that is—I mean maybe you already said this a little bit—but do you think that that is a spatial project or that that's kind of outside [of the realm of a physical design]—i.e. in the way that you handle clients or in the way that you hire people? Is that the "surrounding" part of a project or is that also a spatial idea?

R: I think it's both. It's absolutely both. It's a really difficult thing to try to do something interesting with architecture. I mean we can make really fancy villas for people, and that's a lot of fun to do. Maybe that's my guilty pleasure.

L2: Villas.

R: Just villas. But you know, design for the sake of design is somewhat easy in a way. Design that's trying to engage in the political or social realm—that's not inherently spatial—is difficult. But then again, I feel like, at the same time, so much of our world is understood and organized through space. So it's a matter of finding the right sites, the right places in which things already happen that we can then intervene spatially to redirect flows of people, to redirect observation, to redirect forms of visibility, to make people see things—not to make people see things differently as in some sort of awareness campaign but making people confront spaces, objects, and other people in a designed way. How do we design those kinds of confrontations?

L1: You think it's possible though.

R: Yes, absolutely. It's difficult, it's really difficult when I teach

CONGRATULATIONS!

You made it to page 223.

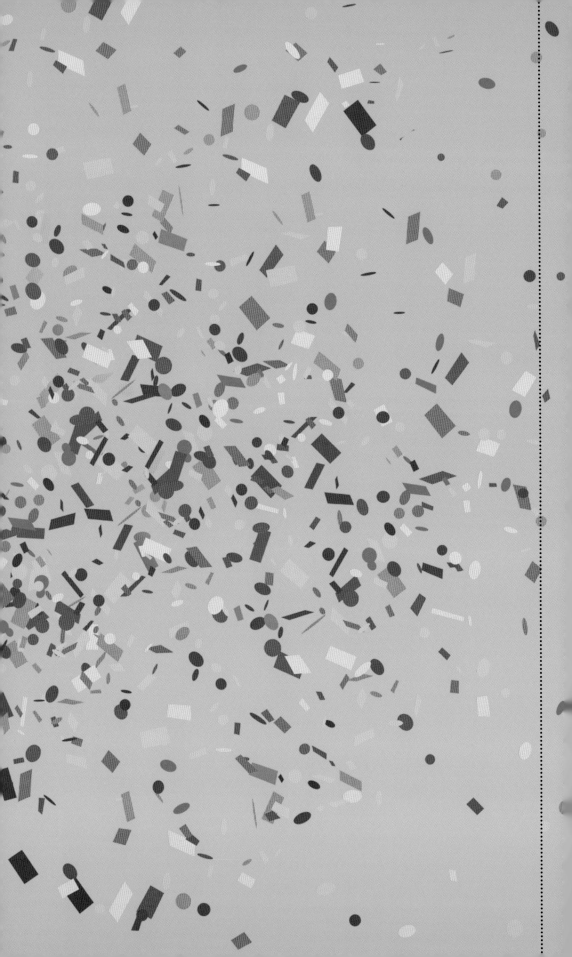

fourth-year students and, you know, we teach a pretty professional form of architecture here at ISU, so when they arrive in my studio it's kind of, uh … there's a period of adjustment. We're not trying to solve a problem, we're not trying to please a client; we're trying to operate within these given networks of people and commodities and capital and I mean that in a literal way, because what we're doing is actually occupying convention centers where people, goods, and capital are constantly flowing and cultural industries and whatever. So that's a way to do it, so we don't occupy some abstract network that only exists in like computers or something.

L2: You were talking earlier about how architecture lags behind. I feel like that's at least partially because it requires a lot of capital to get things off the ground or even to operate on the kind of scale that you would need to operate on to like, whatever, "make a difference." So I don't know if there's a question in there somewhere, but I'm curious when you're teaching these classes do you come at it from a very practical angle? Like who's going to finance the communist revolution?

R: *[laughing]* Yeah. Yeah, that's not going to happen anytime soon.

L2: No, I mean, I can't wait, I mean I feel like—any day now.

R: Well, I mean, I wouldn't advocate that architecture can start a revolution. There's the famous adage from Corbusier, "Architecture or revolution," and I think that pretty much tells the story of architecture: It's at best a reformist liberal practice. It's about making things better! *[general laughter]* of course, within the networks of power and capital that are available, blah blah blah. Today we're in a neoliberal world of private wealth and deprived public expenditure in many cases, so it's not so much about building up the new utopia for the world to come (and you know, I might even argue that utopia as an idea is something that has been realized already—that might be a longer discussion perhaps, but…), so it's about how do we open up new ways of creating discourse about specific issues. That sounds very general and somewhat weak in a way, but it's about creating new forms of visibility about the problems we all know, the problems that are narrated or over-narrated in this sort of, um, uniform way. Again, something like climate change, or even something like capitalism, which I remember a time when I would be reading about capitalism, maybe 12 or so years ago, so not that long ago—and feeling like, to speak about capitalism in public would be like speaking the name of the Lord, or, you know, some kind of taboo really. Today we're very versed in speaking about capitalism in the sort of popular sense. But for that same reason we risk then that the discourse in capitalism gets kind of narrated to us: you know, "well, yes, it's not so great in certain ways and whatever else but you know, it's the only thing there is, right?"

So … I think, you know, forms of resistance today are not only about creating new discourse because discourse and awareness does not lead to transformation by itself. It's also about finding networks of power that can be occupied. And again, the group Not An Alternative is one that has done really brilliant work in this direction. It's an ongoing question and I don't have an answer, but we as architects operate within networks of power and, as you've said, the amount of money that we deal with, the capital that we help to transform into built, fixed capital—real estate and whatever—is substantial, and in that sense, something like mischief is perhaps useful. I'm thinking of Keller Easterling and her suggestions about active and passive form and how the architect should be a kind of mischief-maker to re-code the ways that cities are already coded as software and whatever. So I think that's a viable idea; I'm skeptical to a degree about that because of course it's hard to know when you can occupy this position of being in charge of the code of the production of space. I'm also equally skeptical of like, the civic hacker—which is, again, something that's already produced for us, a subjectivity that we can all inhabit, like "I'm gonna 'hack the system!'" You know, you're like pressing the button that's been made for you to press so that you actually don't press the real buttons that actually affect power.

For me someone like Alberto Toscano, who's a cultural theorist, has been helpful also to think about—what he argues is that we move the site of struggle from locations of production of capital to the choke points in the network of circulation. And that seems interesting. How that actually works, I don't know, but this is sort of what we're trying to do right now.

L2: Yeah, I mean, I think you already said this, but it's kind of a narrative issue, or it's an issue of language in a certain way. And I feel like one of the things that frustrates me about "the discourse" is that, like, we use all of these terms that are sort of ready-made to make us feel subversive, like "We're hacking the system" and there's all this—I feel like it's dropped out of trend a little bit—but the military discourse that people use a lot in architecture where they're, like, "deploying" something.

L1: Like "tactical urbanism."

L2: "Tactical urbanism," all of these things. I feel like there is an uncritical attitude about the language that we use to describe what we're doing.

R: You said the word itself: "doing." We're not supposed to be thinkers; we're supposed to be really well versed in a kind of cocktail-party way where we can impress people with everything that we know. But we're doers in the end, and we're meant to be doers. I'm editing reviews for *The Journal of Architecture* and one of the books that was just reviewed was looking at, um, the notion of inoperativity—I don't know if you're familiar with Giorgio Agamben and his theories but that idea sounds, to me, fascinating: how to make inoperative certain systems or, let's say, points or nodes within networks of power.

Yeah, I mean, I think these are difficult terms because in the end, as architects, as architectural students, whatever, we are already—our practice and our modes of thinking—kind of predicated on the structures of power that make possible architecture as a discourse and practice in the first place. So to try and intervene in systems of capital or state violence or whatever it might be necessarily disrupts those flows of power that make us… work, that give us, you know, professional and, to some degree, academic viability. It's something I'm tremendously frustrated with because we are so conservative. When I was a student—and things are changing, in a really good way but—when I was a student we only had the canon and then, in that sense, "mischief" was the most annoying thing because people were trying to kind of steal terms from other discourses and use them as flowery ways to describe their own design practices and so, you know, my scholarly effort has been to work consistently as much as possible on understanding the connections between space and power specifically with regard to urban infrastructure, domesticity, categories like that. Again I think there's a huge number of people, young scholars in particular who are really doing great work bringing things to light. There's an amazing group called the Feminist Art and Architecture Collaborative who recently published a manifesto in the *Journal of the Society of Architectural Historians*, which is a very conservative journal. And it was amazing to see this three-page manifesto—very powerful way of rejecting the architectural canon and constructing another form of knowledge, a much more open one that's based not on objects but on space and objects, and space as a site of political struggle. It's fantastic work, and there are exciting things happening, but how that translates to practice and then of course how that translates to something that's viable to do as a profession—for you two, and all of your colleagues, once you graduate—that's a real question and one that I would encourage everyone to be thinking about and to find ways that architecture can do more.

I would say one example of an architecture practice that has done that, in a way, is Forensic Architecture. It's the work of Eyal Weizman in London. He set up a thing called the Center for Research Architecture at Goldsmiths. It's a really interesting example of using architectural knowledge, tools, techniques not to build things but to deconstruct and reconstitute war crimes and acts of state violence. It's blossomed into so many other types of investigation [such as] ecological violence, environmental violence, so on and so forth. It's really fascinating stuff.

[long pause]

L1: We're just reviewing our extensive list of questions.

R: What year are you, if I can ask?

L1: We're second-years.

R: Cool, how do you like it?

L1 + 2: *[laughter]*

R: Are you recording right now?

L2: We're recording right now, this is on the record. But it's at our discretion whether or not we write it down.

Who Framed Us?

Esther Leslie

I was once thrown out of my office on Gordon Square by Hollywood. The teams of chunky men, divided between hanging around in clumps or shifting things urgently, took up residence, amidst imported hay bales and cans of paint. A period movie, a comedy version of Sherlock Holmes, was being filmed and the detective—or rather his body double—had to fall from an upper window on the neo-Georgian terrace. He falls out of a window and lands on a pavement, not the pavement that I walk on every weekday, which is of York Stone and suitably consistent with the heritage aims of the area which has led the Hollywood location scouts here in the first place. Laid across this pavement are two meters of fake pavement, sitting atop the usual one, darker in color, raising it a couple of inches off the ground. Perhaps it has a more uniform color, and it has not been stained by chewing gum and municipal bleaches and so provides a more pleasing impression to the audience eye that will drift over it for a fraction of a second. Maybe it is a softer surface—a cartoon pavement that won't damage the stuntman as he falls in the place of the actor. Perhaps he will even bounce, off-camera. It looks like a cartoon pavement. No modulations. Flatly there. It is mobilized for a moment, for as long as it takes to make the stunt happen.

Of course Hollywood manicures reality. It irons out the wrinkles and paints over the blemishes. Never more so than now, with all the computerized and digitized work during production and postproduction that is a key part of all culture industry filmmaking. In doing this, it constructs a hybrid world of actual and virtual impulses. In doing this, it has also prepared the way for new worlds of augmented reality, these vistas in which the real and the virtual co-exist in the same space. Everything is a cartoon now. Everything is an assemblage of the real and the not-quite-real, or real-in-a-different-way, in the way of pixels and programs, but never there, where it is assumed to be. There is, so to speak, a kind of cartoon mischief at work on the surface of the real.

Animation is nowadays a patina that coats our present and will do more so in our futures with projections of enlivened surfaces through various augmented reality systems such as Oculus Rift, Project Morpheus, Magic Leap, OnePlus2, and HTC Vive. Virtual reality technologies, which merge data with real-world environments, fully immerse the viewer-participant. Their uses are in education, training, gaming, entertainment, engineering, design, therapy, retail, pornography. These devices bejewel the landscapes of tomorrow, while also potentially weaponizing them.

Animation in some form or other might train us variously in these new landscapes of "second nature," where we live second lives amidst this new data that is mined, grown, and harvested. Animated landscapes meddle with reality, troubling it in the way that an agitated fluid, a fluid turned turbid, is opaque and screen-like. Goethe described this. Turbidity defines a cloudiness or the presence of particulates, which makes of a substance a *medium*. Turbidity is no obstacle to seeing, as was thought by optical theorists at a time when turbidity was considered a blockage, a fog, a fuzz that obscured things. But Goethe understood that a turbid environment does something to what is seen, mediates it. He glossed "turbidity," from the Latin, as "turbo, turbidity, tobio, trouble"—this agitation makes vision possible in its particularity. Augmented reality is troubled reality: reality made screen-like, turbid, troubled, a world turned surface-for-seeing.

In the future, sceneries, all sceneries, may be exclusively composed of these troubled environments made out of physical materials and virtual data. Or, in the future, those who can find the money for poor bandwidth only, for small data packages, will experience a reality with low-resolution, an unadorned reality, the ungilded or unvarnished truth perhaps. The others, with more spare cash, will enjoy layer upon layer of opacities. This is the biosphere intimated in *Pokemon Go*, in which each environment is an arcade, a video arcade or a shopping one, where the world is a perkier one, co-inhabited by happy little monsters who are keen to be tamed. And yet it is our world, our grids that are triangulated. These grids that are ours are where worldly contradictions, the social relations inside the forms, are hard to perceive or erased or met only as one of the most unexpected elements of the game—an ambush, a sudden sinkhole, the actions of a mischief-maker—which may not have been picked up by the dead eye in the sky that tracks us.

There is, so to speak, a kind of cartoon mischief at work on the surface of the real.

The live action-animated fantasy film *Who Framed Roger Rabbit?* (Robert Zemeckis, 1998), through means that were mainly non-computerized, appears now, projected into this history, as an early example of the tendency to merge actual and virtual. On one plane, if in two separated social environments—one ghettoized, the other dominant—exist the living, breathing humans and the drawn, if no less lively, cartoon characters. Their mischief is one that involves the very crossing of the lines between human world and cartoon world. In the *dénouement*, mischief, which could mean teasing behaviors, cartoon capers, various types of more or less consequential meddling, takes on its full and historic significance. *Mischief*—misfortune or distress, from the old French. To come to an adverse end, as is the fate of the character Judge Doom, steamrollered flat to be what he always actually was—a cartoon character—only then to be dissolved into non-existence.

Who Framed Roger Rabbit? took for granted that humans and animated characters might co-exist in one world. The opening scene is a pastiche of Tom and Jerry cartoons from the 1940s, where cross-species mayhem happens in the kitchen, played by what director Robert Zemeckis called a character with "a Disney body, a Warner head, and a Tex Avery attitude." But it also evokes an early Walt Disney Mickey Mouse cartoon, one of the earliest of all: *Plane Crazy*. From 1928, *Plane Crazy* opens with a scene of Taylorized labor. The demands of labor under new conditions of industrial working life apparently insist that one of the workers (a dachshund) insert himself into the machine, an airplane that Mickey Mouse wants to fly with Minnie Mouse. The dachshund coils himself like an elastic band inside the body of the plane to make it fly. The apparatus—both the one that is the plane and the system of labor that is divided and commanded—is as pitiless as it is amusing for us, the audience. We know that the plane will go out of control: starting, then stopping, then unable to be stopped, as it becomes a vehicle of brutal interpersonal relations.

The mischievousness that typifies the cartoon genre extends into its very frames. It is brought into being, it might be said, by those who have an affinity for the playful. Rumors abound around subtexts in *Who Framed Roger Rabbit?* Some say that early pressings of the Laserdisc of the film had Disney boss Michael Eisner's home phone number on a bathroom wall in Toontown and that Jessica Rabbit is pantless with legs splayed. In another scene, Betty Boop flashes her breast and that *enfant terrible* Baby Herman sticks his finger up a woman's skirt.

Who Framed Roger Rabbit? opens, then, with a cartoon being filmed—as we learn in time, at the point when it goes wrong. Roger Rabbit sees birds instead of stars—that is to say something like, he imagines and brings into being above his head birds instead of the stars that are cartoon-conventional when a blow to the head has occurred. Roger Rabbit, in this sequence, suffers violence: he slips on a rolling pin and soap, burns in the oven, gets electrocuted, gets bashed on the head by pans, tormented by chili sauce, assaulted by knives and a plunger, blown up by a vacuum cleaner, all in the course of working, at one level as a babysitter and at another level as an actor.

But a cartoon character is not vulnerable like a human. A cartoon character is resilient. A cartoon character suffers all this mischief and malice and stands up again, swells out after being flattened, flattens after inflation. Cartoon characters fall out of windows and survive. Roger crashes through a window and leaves behind him a rabbit-shaped cut-out in the venetian blinds. Mischief-makers rarely succumb to mischief. Humans, on the other hand, are vulnerable—and in this film they get pianos or safes dropped on them and they fall from windows and they die.

Though, sometimes, in this film, the rules of the cartoon world do seep out (mischievously) into the proximate human world. Just as there are worlds adjoining—one apparently like ours in terms of physics and logic and one in which the laws of physics and time can be suspended—nothing is absolute. Our private detective survives one flattening. And each one of the rascally cartoon characters is vulnerable in the face of the dip that can dissolve their paint and ink. This all raises the question of origins, or reproduction: social and sexual reproduction. Did these cartoon characters bring themselves into being? Who "framed" Roger Rabbit? Did he make himself or was he made such that he might be unmade again, perhaps by the same vandalizing people who make a freeway or decide that a freeway should be made, thereby changing the whole fate of a town, the presence or absence of an industry and its modes of life, the existence or otherwise of half-lives or non-lives that live, or whatever those mischievous cartoon characters, our *semblables*, are? Our troubled sceneries are beholden to new agents of fate.

In March 2017, in London, a cat food brand, using the CGI skills of JCDecaux's Creative Solutions, set its animated mascot, Felix, some sort of descendant of the original animated moggy Felix the Cat, loose in Waterloo train station in a campaign that involved an Augmented Reality experience. The animated cat leapt between advertisements for other products on the escalator, causing a carefully orchestrated havoc. It swung from clocks, spilled paint, played with a ball, and knocked the sun from the sky. A large screen on the station concourse broadcast interactions taking place between humans and the virtual cat on a platform. People were encouraged to share their hybrid footage on Twitter under the #uptomischief tag. Alex Gonnella, Nestlé Purina's regional marketing director, Northern Region, observed: "Felix is one of the UK's best loved cats, known for his mischievous nature, so it is really exciting to bring that to life through emerging technologies in marketing. We believe the disruptive and interactive nature of the activity we have planned will resonate with consumers in a refreshing and fun way."

Mischief is in the machine, in the machine that is an animal that exports troubles into our world in the shape of a fun that can be purchased and for which we are but props. 🐰

fig. 2 (facing)
Roger Rabbit
(Photo: Ken Lund)

The State of Things is Very Serious.

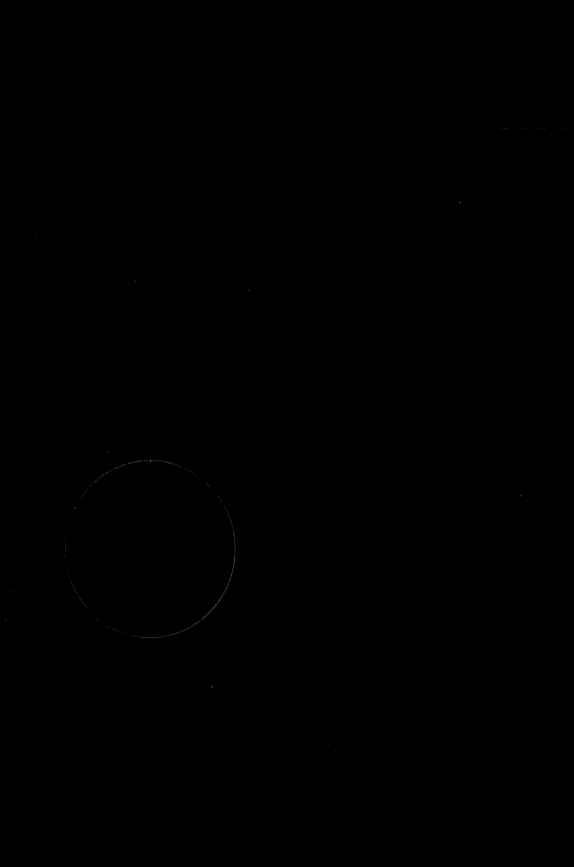

From James A. Teit, "Tahltan Tales:
The Raven Cycle," *The Journal of
American Folklore* 30, no. 18 (1920):
427-273.

"At this time there was no daylight, or sun, moon, or stars. Raven went to a village and asked the people if they could see anything. They said, 'No, but one man has daylight, which he keeps in a box in his house. When he takes off the lid, there is bright light in his house.' The people could not work much, for it was night continually. Raven found out where Daylight Man lived and went to his house. This man also had control of the sun, moon, and stars. Raven went into the house and came out again. He planned what to do to get daylight for himself and the people."

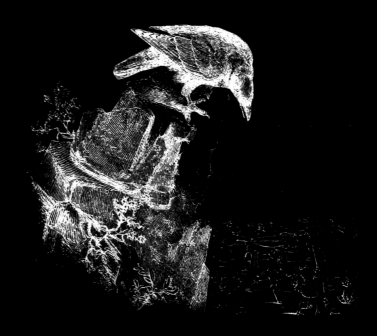

SECTION A CONTINUATION - SOLICITATION/CONTRACT FORM SF 1442 CONSTRUCTION DESIGN/BUILD

SF1442, Block 13a: Offerors shall follow the submittal instructions in Section L of this solicitation to respond to both Phase I - Concept Papers/Request for Qualifications and Phase II - Request for Proposals.

This acquisition will result in the award of multiple IDIQ contracts for the construction of an "Other Border Wall Prototype" with the capacity to issue future task orders for construction along the American-Mexican border. This acquisition is separate and apart from solicitation HSBP1017R0022 for the "Solid Concrete Border Wall Prototype," which is for the acquisition of a prototype using solid concrete materials, in addition to future possible construction along the American-Mexican border.

The performance period of each IDIQ contract shall be five (5) years from date of award with the sum total value of all awarded contracts having a maximum order limit of $300,000,000.

The Government will make the award of each IDIQ contract and the first task order (TO) simultaneously. The first TO award will be for the design and build of the "Other Border Wall Prototype" and Mock-ups (collectively, Prototype) in accordance with the Statement of Work. Award of the Prototype will satisfy the minimum guarantee of the IDIQ contract.

Pursuant to FAR 52.232-18, Availability of Funds, the Government's obligation under this solicitation, or any contract or TO that might result from the solicitation is entirely subject to, and contingent upon, the availability of appropriated funds. No legal liability on the part of the Government shall arise until funds are made available to the Contracting Officer and a TO is awarded by the Contracting Officer. Any offeror proposing on this solicitation does so at its own cost and with the full knowledge that a contract or TO for the Prototype project might not result from this solicitation.

After award of the IDIQ and Prototype TO, the successful IDIQ contractors will all compete for future TOs based upon the evaluation factors set forth in the TO RFPs. Only the successful IDIQ awardees shall be allowed to compete for future TOs under these IDIQs. IDIQ contract holders are expected to submit a proposal for all future TO RFPs received from the Government. However, in the event an awardee is unable to submit a proposal on a particular TO RFP, the contractor is required to notify, in writing, the Contracting Officer who issued the TO RFP within five (5) working days from receipt of the RFP. An awardee can only elect to withdraw from submitting a proposal on three (3) TO RFPs during a 365 calendar day period. Withdrawal requests in excess three (3) in a 365 calendar day period may result in the Government terminating a contractor's IDIQ contract for default.

CONFETTI TIME! 🎉 🎉 🎉 🎉

Make a joyous mess.

Inflatoborder

Rosa Cristina Corrales Rodriguez, Shannon Ruhl, Donna Ryu, and Michelle Stein

The borders we build and their resulting spatial impacts can leave an imprint of division and disunity—a zone of emotional and physical disruption. In times of crisis, these lines have the power to enable a reactive rather than substantive fix to social ills: i.e., put up a wall so tall that only select individuals can cross to the other side. Yet countless scholarly sources tell us that a highly securitized and exclusive border only exacerbates existing relationships of exploitation and discrimination.

The redefinition of borders might result from negotiating terrain, territorial disputes, or newly discovered historical markers. Rather than subjugating a physical structure to adopt the current political or generational agenda, we propose a border that embraces the changing needs of neighboring nations and celebrates diversity through shared initiatives. Exploring opportunities for adaptability and permeability, we reject the border wall as a fetishized object and call for the two nations to live within and around their shared border differently. The result transforms the relationship between Mexico and the U.S. from one of exploitation to one of mutual benefit.

The Inflatoborder provides a place for shared interaction between neighbors, opening opportunities for diplomacy and flexibility at the border zone. Supported by mutual exchange and capitalizing on existing strengths, this user-defined construct encourages communities to come together to share in an activated space. Inflatable and adaptable, the Inflatoborder can continually be re-envisioned according to the desires, needs, and goals of surrounding communities.

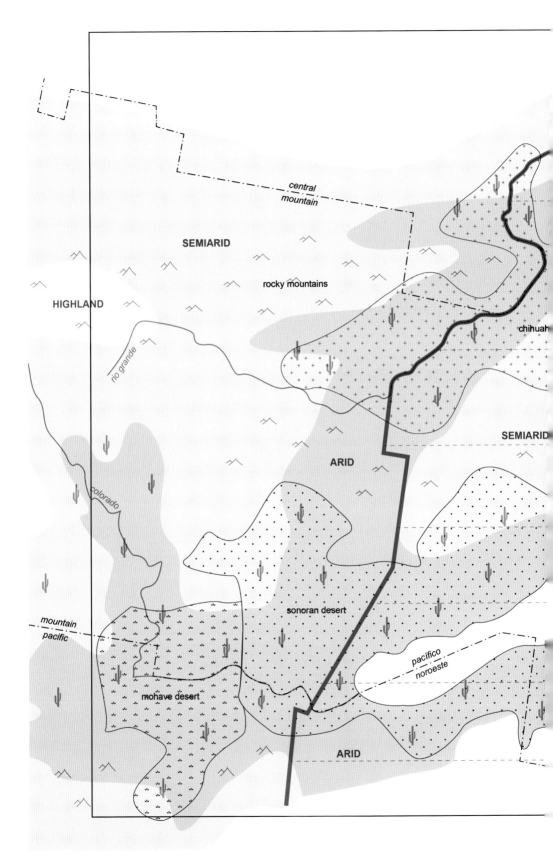

central
mountain

SEMIARID

rocky mountains

HIGHLAND

chihuah

rio grande

SEMIARID

ARID

colorado

sonoran desert

mountain
pacific

pacífico
noroeste

mohave desert

ARID

UNITED STATES

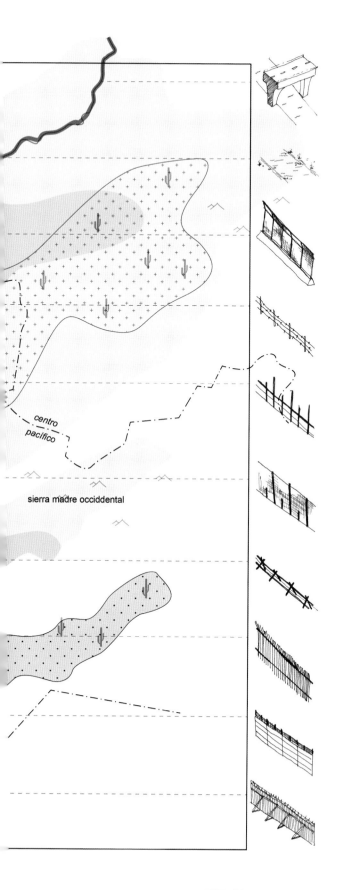

centro
pacífico

sierra madre occiddental

MEXICO

fig. 1
Border Geography: Analysis of the
U.S. and Mexico border.

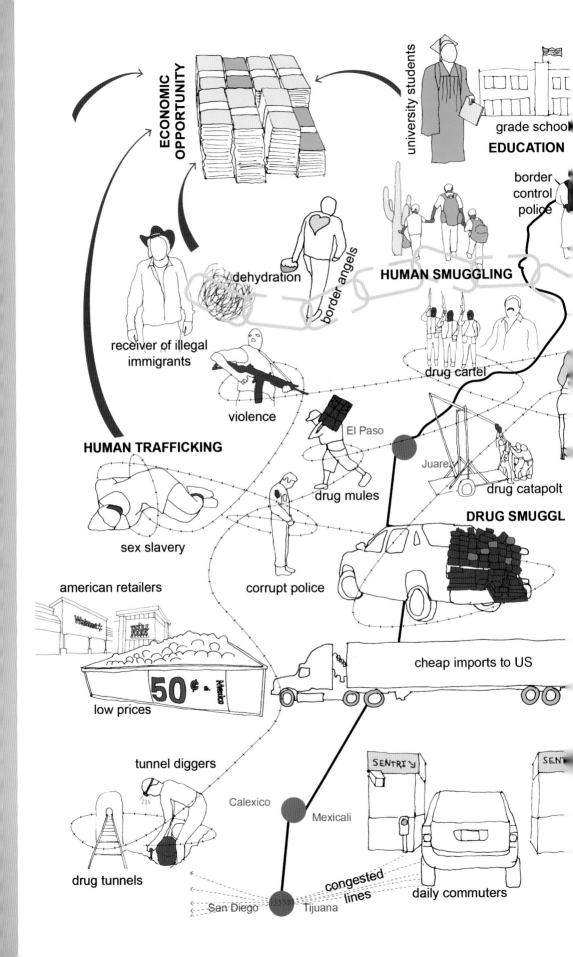

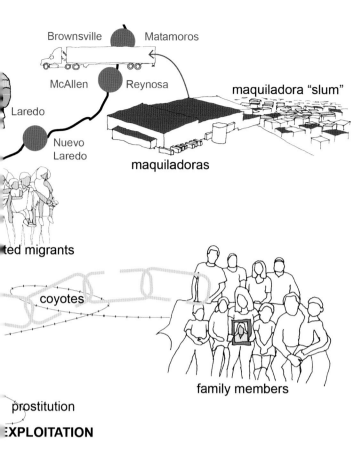

Brownsville   Matamoros

McAllen   Reynosa

Laredo

Nuevo
Laredo

maquiladoras

maquiladora "slum"

ted migrants

coyotes

family members

prostitution

EXPLOITATION

largest amount of cocaine
related deaths

EXPLOITATION OF LABOR

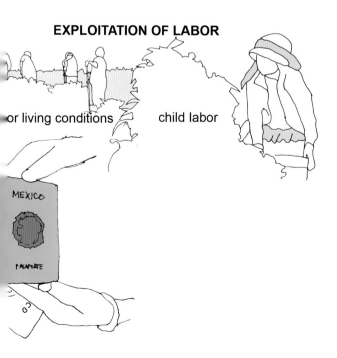

or living conditions   child labor

MEXICO

PASAPORTE

Inflatoborder is comprised of inflatable bubbles situated between infrastructural nodes, retrofitting the material of the existing wall and located at original border monuments. Each bubble is inflated using fans located at the base of the monument node, automated to inflate the membrane to a user-specified air pressure. Depending on the intent, the air pressure can be adjusted to one of three conditions:

1 *Low-pressure system*: the bubble rests on the ground creating an inflated cushion;
2 *Mid-pressure system*: the bubble is occupiable with the membrane acting as an enclosure; and
3 *High-pressure system*: the bubble lifts off the ground and acts as a canopy.

Each node generates energy to power the fans and other resources such as wireless Internet. The means of harvesting energy is determined by site-specific conditions, whether rich in solar, wind, or hydrologic potential. The monument node is a re-appropriation of existing border wall materials including steel tube, chain link, railway ties, and corrugated metal. Recycling existing materials, the proposal reconfigures the lifecycle of the border wall. Where the border traverses agricultural land, an inflatable canopy shades a seasonal roadside market. In dense urban concentrations where public space might be scarce, the whimsical nature of the bubbles attracts children and families to a new bounce-play area. The once-divisive barrier between two countries is now a welcoming, flexible, and shared construct that can be reconfigured and utilized according to the desires, needs, and goals of its local neighbors, instigating a larger change at an international scale. 🐿

Inflatoborder was named a First Place Winner of the 2016 Building the Border Wall? competition.

fig. 3 (facing)
Concept Diagram: Is the border a barrier between two nations ... or an international threshold?

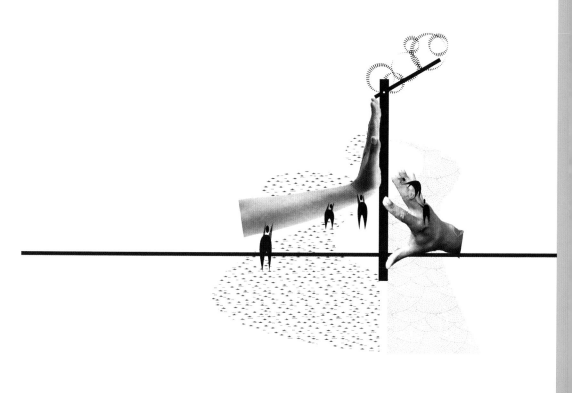

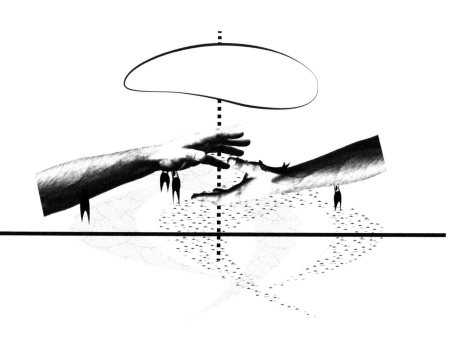

hiker's lookout

internet cafe

market

fishing dock

bridge

picnic shelter

movie theate

"True Reality": The Street as a Critique of Landscape Architecture

Julian Raxworthy

fig. 1 (facing)
A nineteenth-century street of public housing in the (now) inner city suburb of Glebe, in Sydney. Beyond design, decisions in the initial subdivision process about lot size, infrastructure width and development typologies of the market at that time leave a legacy that is self-reinforcing over time. Without requiring design controls, not allowing lot consolidation combined with solar access and lot size effectively manage development operations. Fig trees planted as street trees without a real understanding of their later size now dwarf buildings but not overly large roads, leading to serendipitous errors of predication.

1
Albert Hofmann, *LSD: My Problem Child* (Los Angeles: J. P. Tarcher, 1983), 19.
2
James Corner, "The Agency of Mapping: Speculation, Critique and Invention," in *Mappings*, ed. Denis E Cosgrove (London: Reaktion Books, 1999).

After the world's first acid trip, the accidental maker of LSD, the chemist Dr. Albert Hofmann, described how he "walked out into the garden, in which the sun shone now after a spring rain [and] everything glistened and sparkled in a fresh light." Looking at the landscape around him that he had seen many times, he noted "the world was as if newly created."[1] In lectures on the topic later in life, Hofmann, a Christian teetotaler, suggested that LSD allowed access to "true reality," already all about us but seldom seen. For me, this true reality is the banal, everyday public landscape of the street, which has its own beauty, and which, once examined, exposes the political impotence of landscape architecture. Landscape architecture is impotent because it is located in an ambiguous space between the public and private, between individualism and collectivity, a condition that arises from its complicit role in the capitalist project.

This may seem like an odd claim, because "infrastructure"—an inherently public concept—has never been more celebrated in landscape architecture than it is now. *The Agency of Mapping*[2] spawned a generation of books in a genre that I call "propositional geography," a genre that includes *Taking Measures Across the American Landscape*,[3] *Mississippi Floods*,[4] *Stalking Detroit*,[5] *Reclaiming the American West*,[6] and more recently *Landscape as Infrastructure*.[7] These books direct the attention of the design community toward landscapes that were not ostensibly designed, that exist at the intersection between natural and cultural systems. The scale of these books' attentions was geographic, and their focus was on infrastructure and systems that, despite the rhetorical "agency" of mapping, were outside the scope of what had previously been, and continues to be, landscape architectural practice. Perhaps to compensate for this, elements in more humble projects began to be conceived of and talked about as "infrastructure" that "performed" or was "operative," appropriating the muscularity of geographic language. While this geographic view allowed the uncelebrated functional fabric of the city to be seen, and more importantly, seen in systemic terms, it has proven itself to be observational rather than propositional in terms of real agency in the world. Fetishization or rebranding of infrastructure has not been accompanied by an appreciation of landscape architecture's role as an agent of transformation within the urban economy.

With the aim of valuing it, the environment has been rebranded as "ecosystem services," edited to fit into the logics of capitalism. The designation of the built environment as "infrastructure" has a similar aim. However, recent attention to "green infrastructure" demonstrates the danger of this designation. On the one hand, the category of "green infrastructure" allows the hidden relationship between spaces and systems that have historically been invisible and discrete from one another to be discerned, which in turn allows for enhanced understanding and planning. On the other hand, the identification of such a relationship is just that—identification—and rarely results in action to improve functioning. Indeed, the sheer complexity of a comprehensive green infrastructure system makes it difficult to imagine that the economics of local government and authorities will ever be able to fund it once its scale has been identified. This critique has been previously applied by environmentalists who see "green infrastructure" as primarily rhetorical.[8]

At the same time, the level of novelty expected of landscape architecture projects has increased due to what I would call the "High Line Effect," which, though perhaps the greatest landscape architecture project since Olmsted, is nonetheless an object of high fashion and budget, "where to appreciate the High Line in architectural terms … is to be complicit with the incredible wealth and privilege that built and sustains it."[9] Whereas design was once argued for in terms of its fundamental but often invisible effect on the city, it is now seen more as a normative urban branding factor, such that, in a *mea culpa* moment, fifteen years after his book *The Rise of the Creative Class* had celebrated the influence of "creatives" on developing cities, Richard Florida acknowledged that "the metros with the highest levels of inequality were also those with the most dynamic and successful creative economies."[10] Thus the High Line demonstrates the power of landscape architecture to work in the public realm, while at the same time enhancing economic segregation. But is the High Line really an example of public space? I agree with Bierig that "the idea that [the High Line] is … a 'public' park is part of its myth."[11]

I argue that since public space is everything owned and operated by the state on behalf of the public, projects like the High Line, the new Pershing Square, or any other high-profile "public" projects pale into statistical irrelevance when compared with the sheer linear meters of

3
James Corner and Alex S MacLean, *Taking Measures across the American Landscape* (New Haven: Yale University Press, 1996).

4
Anuradha Mathur and Dillip de Cunha, *Mississippi Floods: Designing a Shifting Landscape* (Yale University Press: New Haven, 2001).

5
Georgia Daskalakis, Charles Waldheim, and Jason Young, eds., *Stalking Detroit* (Barcelona: ACTAR, 2001).

6
Alan Berger, *Reclaiming the American West* (New York: Princeton Architectural Press, 2002).

7
Pierre Bélanger, *Landscape as Infrastructure* (New York: Routledge, 2017).

8
Hannah Wright, "Understanding Green Infrastructure: The Development of a Contested Concept in England," *Local Environment: The International Journal of Justice and Sustainability* 16 (2011): 1003–19.

9
Aleksandr Bierig, "The High Line and Other Myths," *Log 18*, Winter 2010 (2010): 132.

10
Richard Florida, *The New Urban Crisis: Gentrification, Housing Bubbles, Growing Inequality and What We Can Do About It* (London: One World, n.d.), xxii.

11
Ibid., 134.

street in the public realm. Yet the everyday street is incidental to trends in landscape design, despite having the biggest impact on people's lives. The street is the interface into all other places into the city and is the foreground to any aesthetic of the urban or architectural project. So why is it generally ignored by landscape architects? I propose in this essay that there are two interconnected reasons that the street is ignored: one, because the street is political; and two, because the street operates at the nexus of planning and design.

Public Space Is Political

To focus on the street as a public space means to understand the role of the state and its purview, and it is here that a key contradiction arises for landscape architecture. Situated in a no-man's land between the public and the private, landscape architecture cannot help but be complicit no matter what occurs: if it's working for the market, its relation to landscape systems is revealed as token, since its values will have to be sacrificed to the individual client; if it's working for the state, then its claims to the social aspect of the market, as a collective of individuals, is revealed as insincere since it will always have to choose the greater good over the individual. Capitalism is thus a key factor because contemporary democracy is tied to the idea of the autonomy of the individual and private property.

Since, as David Harvey noted, "we live … in a world in which the rights of private property … trump all other notions of rights,"[12] the sanctity of private property under the capitalist system severely impinges on landscape architecture's ability to achieve its social, environmental, and design ambitions. Landscape architecture's political impotence, its fear of taking a political position in relation to its disciplinary aims, can be demonstrated by comparing the degree to which a key article of the last ten years—Harvey's "The Right to the City"—has been referenced in architectural publications but rarely, if at all, in those of landscape architecture.[13] Instead, landscape architecture's political position is inferred through its "environmentalism," a neo-liberal cause-célèbre that was once leftist but has become as inherently conservative as conservationist. Meanwhile, property speculation—a key process for landscape architects—carves up and reorganizes land according to a blockchain-like history of transactions. While the cadastral process may at times negotiate around topographic or hydrological features, it typically operates in an abstract economic realm.

Street as Algorithm

Considering the relationship between private property and the public is key to a discussion of the street. This relationship affects the way that we approach the design process, moving from design as direct formal proposition to design as policy and code. In streetscape design studios, I ask students first to define the site, the most basic starting point, which I refer to as "room to move." Although the site boundary is visible, students will inevitably start to coopt front yards into service of their design, rather than sticking to the road easement.[14] When asked how

12
David Harvey, "The Right to the City," *New Left Review*, 2008, 23.

13
To make this claim I undertook a reasonably thorough search of Google Scholar for "Landscape architecture" and "Right to the City." I would welcome, and indeed seek out, any writing on this topic that could be referred to me.

14
I am setting the students up here, but it is an important lesson, and more importantly, a research interest of mine.

they will affect this change to private properties, they become vague, unsure of what political and planning tools might be necessary for such a proposition.

It is at this point that I introduce the idea that achieving strategic objectives requires not just design in the formal sense, which the material design of the easement would include (since it assumes one client, whether the municipality or the developer), but policy, which would allow design to reach into the private lot—an essentially political ambition. Considering the street in relation to private property makes streetscape design about policy or code because all owners must be treated fairly and equally in the realm of governance. Planning policy must be fair, transparent, and universal under democratic governance; it must also be able to operate around diverse individual situations, building over time, so that "like genetic code in biology, standards are the functional and physical unit of planning legacy, passed from one generation to another."[15] Code is the interface between those abstract policies and designed outcomes, "legal and moral instruments by which professionals can guarantee the good of the public."[16]

Treating design as code is not about surrendering form; rather, it is a different way of working with it. I call this approach "working at a remove": that is, creating conditions for particular formal outcomes to arise. Even where urban coding is not the aim, this way of thinking has value since it precipitates a catalytic approach. In studios I encourage students to work iteratively back and forth from their proposition, where the initial design is analyzed for principles that can be articulated as rules or parameters to be applied to another test site, recognizing that any outcome is provisional and contingent.[17] In my recent teaching I have been exploring parametric urbanism using Grasshopper to visualize the syntax and effects of such rules. As Michael Sorkin argues in *Local Codes,*[18] the textual nature of policy and codes actually allows room for designer interpretation, leading to a diverse city with perceptible general outlines. Rather than being "designs" per se, the resultant forms are better referred to as "performative envelopes."

In landscape architecture, there has been an increasing interest in working in Global South contexts and "advocacy." However, I argue that operating in both these contexts as a political alternative to working locally reveals landscape architecture's political impotence by preferring symptoms to causes, despite being a discipline that is about the latter. In the first instance, the parlous state of many Global South cities is caused by global capital—the refuge of landscape architecture—and in the second, to advocate is to have already surrendered any real power. In conclusion, I propose that landscape architecture look to planning rather than architecture, which landscape architecture has been mimicking for the last 20 years, for an approach to working with cities. Rather than focus on "catalytic" projects that are treated as objects, complicit with capitalist systems of gentrification, it should operate across the city as territory, proposing speculative policy that positively operates for all citizens, the street once more a zone to celebrate the civic. 🐰

fig. 2 (facing)
Increasing density in Melbourne requires increases in floor area ratios which in turn necessitates the requirement to allow consolidation and in turn height, but zero setback and consideration of the proportion of the street width to building height allows for both some degree of invention and maintaining core street qualities that demonstrate the suburbs social and development history, as layers are maintained and revealed in controlled juxtaposition.

15
Eran Ben-Joseph, *The Code of the City: Standards and the Hidden Language of Place Making* (Cambridge, Massachusetts: The MIT Press, 2005), xiii.

16
Ben-Joseph, xiv.

17
Anyone familiar with my research in my PhD will recognize that this is the same approach I propose for dealing with gardens (Julian Raxworthy, "*Novelty in the Entropic Landscape: Landscape Architecture, Gardening and Change*" (University of Queensland, 2013).

18
Michael Sorkin, *Local Codes* (Cambridge, Massachusetts: The MIT Press, 1993).

The Politics of the Graft

Margaretha Haughwout | Guerrilla Grafters

Guerrilla Grafters

Guerrilla Grafters graft fruit bearing branches onto publicly accessible, sterile fruit trees that are used on city streets for ornamental purposes. We work in broad daylight at the cusp of spring. In the Bay Area, this is when February turns to March, and in New York trees begin to wake up in April. Grafting tools, wax, special tape, and branch tips the length of fingers are what we tote along; but ladders, buckets of water, loppers, small animals, curious friends, and eager beginners can also be a part of our coterie. We feel so conspicuous when we congregate with tools that wound and heal around the smooth, bare trees, but then again, we move fast. We keep a lookout—down the high-end streets with fresh, colorful paint where everyone walks around with delicate shopping bags and also down the streets where people sleep on the sidewalks during the day (often, these are one and the same). Most of the time, passers-by do not ask us what we are doing, though Guerrilla Grafters do facilitate relations with neighbors of the grafted tree whenever we can.

Guerrilla grafting—this act of artistic rebellion—reveals the reach of support for a vision of the urban commons, spaces of care that collapse divides between capitalist agriculture, its subsequent ownership regimes, and resource-rich systems of multi-species collaboration. The gesture of the graft and the graft as sculpture draw from rich histories of avant-garde, and socially-engaged art practices, ushering forth a set of dynamic material relations that interrogate binaries of nature and culture, public and private, imagining city streets as delicious and resilient.

Material Gestures

A good graft is artful and precise. Our wedge grafts are carefully executed on thin tree branches with thin branch cuttings (called "scions") that match in size. The tree branch is cut into a V, and the scion is shaped into a matching arrow (^) on two sides. As the grafter connects these, she is careful to match up the green cambium layer on both branch and scion, which is between the dead inner wood and the outer bark, where water and sugar travel. From dormancy to life again, the fruit tree forms buds and this is when a graft is most likely to take. There is one grafter per branch, though it is helpful to have an assistant hold the surgical materials. There could be a third on lookout or for any other tagging that is to be done: secret graffiti codes marking the territory, or QR and RFID tags for additional information about the tree, the graft, or the hidden neighborhood commons more generally.

We identify three aspects of our material labor: daring, caring, and sharing. The dare is the moment of the graft. Like graffiti, which has the same etymology, grafting is considered vandalism in San Francisco, the city where this project first emerged.[1] The San Francisco Department of Public Works declares our work illegal, but we see our work as a political graft as well. Our work is termed as guerrilla because it is covert, laterally organized. It is the work of the dare.

Often, we find that a tree needs extra water or needs a pruning when we are conducting a graft. If we can, we prune branches in order to increase air and light through the limbs. Once a tree has been grafted (ideally with more than one graft), it must then be watched patiently. These are the stages of caring. When the grafted branches bloom and leaf out, the grafter knows the scions have taken; the tree has accepted the branch as its own and is delivering water and sugar through that layer of green between the bark and the wood. The grafter might now find a nearby neighbor to care for the tree while the branch matures enough to bear fruit. It usually takes two to five years for a grafted branch to mature. We have seen grafts bear fruit immediately (as with a successful pear graft in San Francisco that fruited within five months of attachment), but usually grafts require abeyance. City dwellers who heard rumors of Guerrilla Grafters in 2012 might be surprised in 2020 to see a transformed and more participatory streetscape.

Why are property owners, the very rich, and city governments so opposed to a city abundant in fruit?

Distributed relationships are relationships of care that coordinate harvests and offer proof of concept against the vehement opposition expressed by city government about people slipping on fallen fruit, or that fruit trees on city streets attract rats and the houseless. The Guerrilla Grafters invite designs for nets at the bases of trees that collect fallen fruit, and celebrate gleaners that harvest and redistribute fruit. We want to interrogate why city agencies and other proponents of property suggest a hungry person eating on the street beside a tree should be prohibited through the propagation of sterility. Pairing houseless people with rats (a pairing that

1

Ian Pollock, conversation with the author, October 2011.

has happened in conversation with property owners or San Francisco city agencies and Guerrilla Grafters on more than one occasion) reflects a deeply problematic hierarchy of human, subhuman, and non-human, and reinforces environmental injustice across many species. This hierarchy rests on a binary of nature and society that justifies capitalism's process of cheapening certain lives.[2] Lateral relationships and connections across species intervene in this binary and lay the groundwork for how Guerrilla Grafters seek to foster acts of sharing through pollinators, companion species, and distribution models.

We see the graft as a set of branching material gestures with many branching responses.[3] Daring provokes caring which in turn elicits sharing. The attention to the tree's branches in early spring brings about watering and pruning for example. As fruit ripens, another set of material actions—gleaning and distribution—come about. These embodied actions provoke larger sites of contestation about resource management and what kinds of relationships can best create abundance and resiliency for human and non-human city residents.

Performance of Scarcity

The guerrilla graft is a kind of socially-engaged art practice that purposefully toys with frame and form in order to emphasize dynamics and process, including a range of reactions to the gesture of the graft and its implicit proposal for free fruit. When cities declare this artistic labor an act of vandalism, this declaration becomes a kind of performance that is subject to analysis.[4] Rather than our position only being brought into a set of legal and capitalistic narratives, we bring them into our story, our theater. The gesture of the graft invokes a celebration and a fight. There is a collective "yes" that emerges from the idea of ingesting one's city and engaging it in ways that do not involve having to make a purchase, and a resounding "no" that emerges from city agencies revealing themselves to be in service to the mechanisms of ownership and profit. Our protagonists celebrate propagation, replication, juice, encounters, edible cities, resilience. We ask: why are property owners, the very rich, and the departments in city government they influence (all fruit eaters, presumably) so opposed to a city abundant in fruit?

Staging the Class Struggle

The gesture of the guerrilla graft generates what Augusto Boal called the discursive theater. Boal proposes a kind of theater for the people that collapses the proscenium and uses sites of daily life as the stage. Boal sees that this kind of theater never ends and is a kind of continual rehearsal. In this kind of theater, we ask why people do the things they do, and how we can rehearse a different world. "Contrary to the bourgeois code of manners," says Boal, "the people's code allows and encourages the spectator to ask questions, to dialogue, to participate."[5] In this kind of theater, we see tension and fights as class commentary. The better the fights, the more passionate the positions, the better we have done our jobs. Everyone involved becomes an artist and a performer.

2

Jason W. Moore, *Capitalism in the Web of Life: Ecology and the Accumulation of Capital* (London and New York: Verso, 2015).

3

This use of the term "gesture" is inspired by Ricardo Dominguez. See Ricardo Dominguez, "Gestures," in *Live: Art and Performance*, ed. Adrian Heathfield (New York: Routledge, 2004), 72-75.

4

See for example Amy Crawford, "Renegade arborists creating forbidden fruit in San Francisco," *SF Examiner*, January 4, 2012, http://www.sfexaminer.com/sanfrancisco/renegade-arborists-creating-forbidden-fruit-in-san-francisco/Content?oid=2189270.

5

Boal, Augusto. *Theater of the Oppressed* (New York: Theater Communications Group, 1985), 142.

In San Francisco, there are more and more folks with all their belongings in shopping carts or with their shopping carts filled with bottles and more and more tech workers with expensive shoes and no one in between. We walk down the streets of San Francisco and see rich people spending $10 on a scoop of "homemade" cherry ice cream right beside an ornamental cherry tree. The houseless are not considered citizens by the new tech elite: "in other cosmopolitan cities, the lower part of society keep to themselves. They sell small trinkets, beg coyly, stay quiet, and generally stay out of your way. They realize it's a privilege to be in the civilized part of town and view themselves as guests. And that's okay," said a CEO new to San Francisco in 2012.[6] The city and its elite invoke specters of danger, disgust, and disease in order to distract people from the real problems of property ownership and consolidation of wealth by the very few.

The practice of guerrilla grafting is a performance of abundance that reveals the legally sanctioned, and legally enforced, performance of scarcity that we participate in daily in the U.S. This forms a context for contestation over what the city should be and who may or may not benefit. One could also see the graft as a metaphor for the linking up of ideas that shift the flow of nutrients: in this scenario, local government is a sterile tree.

Physical Site, Imaginative Site: Artaud's Haunting Theater

Much of this ecological and social theater happens in the imagination. This imaginative theater could also invoke Antonin Artaud. Artaud says "in the true theater a play disturbs the senses' repose, frees the repressed unconscious, incites a kind of virtual revolt (which moreover can have its full effect only if it remains virtual), and imposes on the assembled collectivity an attitude that is both difficult and heroic."[7]

We imagine the graft bearing fruit when we attach green wood. We imagine an encounter with difference that could be an encounter of repair. Disembodied bureaucrats in the mediascape imagine a civilized member of society slipping on cherries that have fallen on the sidewalk amidst the houseless getting munched on by rats and dying of the plague. Guerrilla Grafters argue that these specters are meant to turn us away from an engagement with the landscape of our city and each other. But we celebrate all these imaginings and their conflicts—we embrace these conflicts as part of our theater. We are grateful to the fearless arts that support and stage conflicts—between grafters and property owners, between various kinds of fruit eaters, between fruit eaters and city officials—because democracy does not exist without difference. Facilitating an encounter allows for an ethic of difference, and, as Deborah Bird Rose points out, drawing on Emmanuel Levinas, ethics precede ontology. Our lives are determined by ethics that are "situated in bodies and in time and in place."[8]

The graft is a material sculpture, and it results in a set of changes, potentials, and exchanges in eco-social relations. And so, we also draw from Joseph Beuys' idea of Social Sculpture, where "art is now the only

fig. 2 (previous spread)
Grafting Demo: Make sure to line up the cambium layer, the thin layer of green between the outer bark, and the dead inner wood.
(Photo: Margaretha Haughwout)

6
Sam Biddle, "Happy Holidays: Startup CEO Complains SF Is Full of Human Trash," *Valley Wag*, December 11, 2012, http://valleywag.gawker.com/happy-holidays-startup-ceo-complains-sf-is-full-of-hum-1481067192.

7
Antonin Artaud, *The Theater and its Double* (New York: Grove Press, 1958), 24.

8
Deborah Bird Rose, *Reports from a Wild Country: Ethics for Decolonization* (Sidney: University of New South Wales Press, 2004), 8.

9

Joseph Beuys, "I am Searching for a Field Character," in *Participation*, ed. Claire Bishop (Cambridge: MIT Press, 2006), 125-127.

evolutionary-revolutionary power. Only art is capable of dismantling the repressive effects of a senile social system to build a social organism as a work of art."[9] The sculpture is the grafted tree, governance in relation to the more-than-human, as well as viable, cultivated, mutually beneficial relations with the life that surrounds us.

The graft itself is a performance and a sculpture, and it results in a set of material propositions for anti-capitalist, or post-capitalist changes, changes that require an understanding of society to include the more-than-human. It begins with a branch.

Creating / Cultivating a Way Out

10

Ian Pollock, conversation with the author, June 2014.

We have this idea for the city, the pinnacle of capitalist civilization, with its resource drain and resultant stratification, to be a site where we move from sterility to fruit, from scarcity to abundance, from the blank sidewalk to graffiti tag, from urban enclosure to urban commons, from winter to spring.[10] Most cities in late capitalist North America are sterile trees. The idea of grafting a fruiting scion onto a sterile tree seems to match this idea we have for the city. We understand the city to facilitate the continual thieving from humans and non-humans living in precarity; an agriculture that fetishizes annual mono-crops is a principal prerequisite for this theft. To create and tend to a more-than-human commons in the city is to begin to stanch the enormous suck of resources drained from the surrounding countryside and from far-off countries. To graft onto the sterile city is to tap into this flow and redirect it, reimagining different kinds of cultivations where people and land are "good medicine for each other."[11]

11

Robin Wall Kimmerer, *Braiding Sweetgrass: Indigenous Wisdom, Scientific Knowledge, and the Teaching of Plants* (Minneapolis: Milkweed Editions, 2013).

The fruit tree operates as a mythological and technological doorway between different conceptions of nature-cultures. It often figures at the cusp of a transition from shared and resilient models of existence to models of control and ownership. It appears in the Old Testament tale of the Garden of Eden, and again during enclosure, when thorny hawthorn and tangled elder (once central allies in the peasant commons) line the hedgerows in England dividing up and obliterating the commons, literally driving commoners to the city for work (but also feeding them along the way). The fruit tree can herald us away from capitalist civilization: hawthorn, in fact, makes a great stock tree. When we eat the fruit again, it is evident that there is a range of bioregionally and historically specific strategies for cultivation and forage that result in radically different eco-social formations. Let's start with Bing Cherries and head toward rooftops and vertical gardens teeming with wild strawberries, thimbleberries, wild grapes; manzanita cider and mashed gooseberry.

Techniques for Abundance

The Guerrilla Grafters know that certain human gestures can enhance resilient and beneficial ecologies, and that controlling the wild, erasing it, or marking it off as untouchable lays the groundwork for political formations unable to resist forces of greed. As M. Kat Anderson writes,

fig. 3 (facing)
A pear graft fruits in an undisclosed location. (Photo: Britta Leijonflycht)

12
M. Kat Anderson, *Tending the Wild* (Berkeley: University of California Press, 2005), 3.

13
Bird Rose, *Reports from a Wild Country*, 23-30.

14
Hayden White, "Bodies and Their Plots" in *Choreographing History*, ed. Susan Leigh Foster (Bloomington: Indiana University Press, 1995).

a "concept of California as unspoiled, raw, uninhabited nature— as wilderness—erase[s] the indigenous cultures and their histories from the land and dispossess[es] them of their enduring legacy of tremendous biological wealth."[12] Conceptions of nature as pristine or "unspoiled" make gestures of repair and "recuperation," to use Deborah Bird Rose's term, impossible.[13] These gestures are essential for acts of worlding that unravel colonial and capitalist ways of being and knowing. Certain simple gestures can produce encounters of infinite complexity and biodiversity. Attracting new human and non-human fruit eaters as a result of our grafts means incorporating new design elements—a tall pole to attract an owl or a hawk (to address the issue of too many rats), expanded permeable surface around the tree, and underplantings of daffodils, yarrow, and borage, for instance. We look at the ground we stand on and to those working along the edges of, or outside of capitalist civilization for alliances, technologies, and modes of engagement that unravel capitalist "plots" (agricultural plots, conspiratorial plots, historical plots).[14]

Grafting is a skilled performative and sculptural gesture to cut branches in a way that makes more branches, to attach branches that make fruit and viable pollen, to engage in relationships that fold economic divisions and redistribute abundance. What we wish to show is that scarcity is a condition of capitalism, and our performance/sculpture points to a way out, a very tiny step among many, of this condition, a condition that fundamentally relies on binaries of nature and culture, public and private. Guerrilla Grafters encourage looking at neighborhoods of more-than-human life in ways that generate resources rather than deplete them, from sunlight falling on rooftops, to coppiced ash for buildings and pathways that make for healthier trees, to deadheading plants like *Hypericum perfolatum*—a practice which makes more blossoms—for medicine. Guerrilla Grafters think that all artists—everyone—should make this kind of labor the center of their practice so that our earth, and our cities especially, become laboratories for survival. 🐰

"A Question of Life or Death": A Chat with Rintala Eggertsson

The Editors

fig. 1 (facing)
Dagur (left) and Sami (right) hold boards for scale at the beginning of their building workshop at the University of Virginia School of Architecture.
(Photo: Leah Grossman)

Sami Rintala and Dagur Eggertsson were visiting professors at the University of Virginia School of Architecture in the fall of 2017. The following interview dates from the final week of their three-week design-build workshop, during which students designed and built a wood pavilion on UVA grounds (fig. 4).

Sarah (L1): Every word you say is now recorded.

Dagur Eggertsson (D): My throat is very dry.

L1: We're going to get some beer. It'll help.

Maddie (L2): So, who is more serious?

Sami Rintala (S): Depends on the situation.

L1: In a serious situation.

D: It's a contagious thing.

L2: Seriousness is contagious?

D: I think it is in many ways …

——

Waitress: Y'all ready to order?

fig. 2
Corte del Forte
Venice Biennale, 2018
(Photo: Rintala Eggertsson)

L1: Y'all know what you want?

S: Green Flash sounds nice. I'll take one.

Waitress: So, two Green Flashes?

S: Yeah.

Waitress: *[counting around the table]* Three, four, five.

S: Perfect.

—

D: So, back to the question. I think that when you are starting to develop work relationships, humor is actually what attracts people to work together. I think it's kind of easy to become irritated and agitated over how you are working, so I think that's one thing that was immediately very easy and simple between the two of us. We were not taking things way too seriously. But with humor, comes also the opposite side, there is also seriousness … maybe it's kind of a seriousness of life that comes with architecture. Things you have to deal with—situations. So yeah, architecture can be a question of life or death but there has to be a way of going about it with humor and looking at things from a side view. You have to zoom out and see things from a different perspective.

fig. 3
Land(e)scape
Savonlinna, Finland
1999
(Photo: Rintala Eggertsson)

D: Sami … are you being too serious?

S: I think there is nothing really that one should be very serious about in life.

L2: Nothing?

S: Nothing. It's a big joke, the whole thing, in a way. It's a kind of paradoxical, humorous thing—the whole humanity—and architecture along with it. So, why should we be very serious about it? Because it's full of paradoxes all the time. It's better just to find your own jokes among those. I think we have a nice way of making stories about our projects. I like that very much, because it makes meaning in life. And without this kind of poetry of what has to happen anyway, what's the meaning of anything really? So, you just make your own small poems about every situation … can be humorous or tragic or anything. But, for sure it's not serious. That's an invented issue, the whole thing.

L2: There's a quote—do you know Hannah Arendt, the philosopher?

D: Oh, yeah.

L2: She has a quote that's like, in a way, um, comedy approaches the human condition more seriously than tragedy,[1] and it kind of reminds me about what you were saying—nothing is serious. And that's part of why we were talking about "mischief" as the theme of the journal …

1
This is a misquote of Hannah Arendt quoting Bertolt Brecht; the full quote is "One may say that tragedy deals with the sufferings of mankind in a less serious way than comedy," and can be found in a 1974 interview with Roger Errera, published here: http://www.nybooks.com/articles/1978/10/26/hannah-arendt-from-an-interview/.

fig. 4 (facing)
Pavilion designed and built by UVA
students during a workshop led by
Rintala Eggertsson as part of Seth
McDowell's Fall 2017 design-build
studio
(Photos: Esteban Chavez, Calvin
Heimberg)

—

Waitress: Okay, some Green Flashes.

L2: Perfect timing.

S: We were just trying to be serious.

[laughter]

Waitress: Okay, two more. Pass this back.

—

L2: So, one of the reasons we were talking about doing "mischief" for the journal is because we feel like in design school, in particular, the environment is very serious. We talk about problems a lot. And we talk about solving problems a lot, but, in a way, solving problems is not our job or it's not why a lot of us came to the field. This attitude about solving the problem is getting in the way of having a creative thought about the world. We're interested in hearing your thoughts on that because it seems like you have a similar perspective. Where do you think architecture fits between being a public service and an art? How do you navigate that kind of divide?

D: Our professor, Juhani Pallasmaa, said it's not interesting to answer questions, but to define the questions. I think that's, in many ways, a key issue—that we have to be able to rephrase the questions that are constantly being asked about things. It's easy to end up in a situation where you are constantly being the expert and answering all the questions. There's a certain sport that develops within the field where people are trying to be the best at answering the questions about energy use in buildings, ecology, structural solutions. And I think that connects us with the way the role of the architect has been defined through the ages as being at the top of the hierarchy. Whereas we are now in a society where the architect isn't coming from high up in the hierarchy. We are more or less middle-class people who are working with everybody. We need to redefine that role, in many ways, so that we can communicate with people from all kinds of classes, from everywhere in society. I think that is actually a much more meaningful role to play, because you get a whole new source of inspiration. Participation is one way that is helping redefine the question in my opinion.

S: Very nice answer. I think also the question is a good question, but it's a little bit, uh, distant. Now, everyone is travelling and using the Internet and knowing much more about everybody's culture and the cultures are mixing and there's much more interference. Every profession is changing, and architecture may be one of the most changing professions. And maybe our first reaction is that it becomes this "star architecture" culture where some architects get these kinds of big jobs in Dubai and make signature buildings. But that's just the first reaction. I think more interesting, maybe, is what happens now when not only 100 architects start making these buildings, but 100,000. And they start making normal buildings in each other's cultures. And that's your generation. So, you should think differently. The previous generation is lost, because they only think of form, money, and these things, which are lost causes already. It's more about concept and working together, so there's a lot of hope. It's not about the highest class doing those things, but what happens when the normal architects start making for normal people, normal things in life and make that culture higher? So, I think this is just the first reaction now. And now it's gone and everybody's tired of it. So, what's the next step? It will be interesting to see.

D: Architects tend to cling on to the "hero" idea. It's very hard for the architecture organizations to let go of that image, because they are fighting for better salaries or good positions in urban development projects. And the best way, as they have defined it, is to maintain this "expert" role in the processes. So, it will take a while to break down those patterns, and I'm not sure if you need to make a revolution and break down all kinds of barriers, but I think that our answer has been to widen up and offer another approach—with dialogue, with user participation. Almost to a degree to where people are a bit scared of whether or not the creative role will vaporize and disappear. And that becomes the—how do you say—least common denominator that defines the projects. But I think that as good architects, you have to be in charge and you have to collect the vectors and point them in a direction where things have to go. And that's why we often say we are more often pedagogues than architects, meaning experts. Some friends of ours say that they are more sociologists. That's another way of putting it. Collecting information— feedback—from people and enabling them to become participants and helping them to shape their societies. I think that's one thing that your generation is, in many ways, meeting—a society which is partly closed to participation. Where does decision-making take place? That's a very big question and most people don't have the answers. It happens somewhere in town council or in some contractors' offices and that's, in my opinion, very anti-democratic. I think that's a problem that we have in society today—that decision-making takes place very far away from people. How can we turn it around? I think if we continue like this we will have generations of people that just don't care about how things happen. If the road goes in this or that direction—it's somebody else who decides those things.

L2: Or you get an insurrection, right?

D: A what?

L2: Or you get a revolution. You get one or the other. You get people who don't care or you get the opposite.

D: Right, there is a sort of rising awareness of things. I think that's the closest we can come to revolution in today's society.

L2: Well, in America, definitely.

fig. 5 (facing)
SALT Festival pavilion
(Photo: Marte Antonsen)

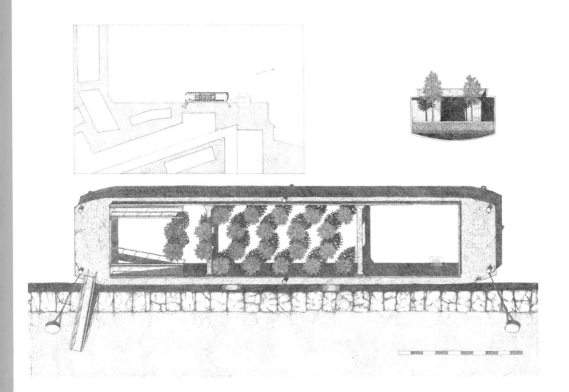

D: People are very conformed. But there is another kind of revolution going on, where people are becoming more aware and more critical about things. And I think that's very positive.

L2: So, it seems like you're saying the role of architect is becoming less of a top-down-imposing-your-ideas-on-society and more about facilitating.

S: I think that architects have no power whatsoever at the moment in the building industry. You can have very nice positions if you have a good client, who is driving you and cooperating with you. But, if you participate in the general mass production of buildings—which is maybe 90% of everything—it's very difficult for an architect to decide much. So, I think it's also a nice survival strategy for new architects to think about how to be a different kind of architect who makes things a different way. So, instead of competing with the same methods you should make your own methods. Nobody has ever agreed how an architect works in reality. There could be very different ways of making architecture. That's your main product anyway. Build a house. How to get that done in a different way than the one which is obvious could be a good question, too. I have found it very difficult to make, for instance, public houses, in the normal way as an architect. I don't think that I'm the worst architect in the world, I'm not the best either. But still, I haven't gotten any public buildings so far. There's some sort of glass roof for just being an honest architect and trying to make good architecture. So, you have to break that glass roof with your own tactics if you think you have something good to offer people.

fig. 7
Built pavilion
Sixty Minute Man
Venice Biennale, 2000
(Photo: Rintala Eggertsson)

But, of course, there's a lot of really good architects who make it anyway, with the system that is there. I really respect that. We visited one yesterday. There's people who make beautiful houses. But, usually, if you look at cities—what's being done—all the things that are popping up; there's nothing you can even call "architecture" anymore. We just close our eyes and think that this is normal because "that just happens everywhere." It doesn't need to be so. We are kind of played out a little bit out of the main theater of action. We are just a curiosity for museums and churches. I exaggerate a little bit to make my point.

L2: What is good architecture?

[laughter]

S: It's something that people like so much that they take care of it and it lasts for a very long time. So, it stays as a cultural heritage because people love it so much that they either want to live in it or work in it or just take care of it because they think it's so important.

L2: What if they hate it at first?

S: That's usually what happens with new architecture, because architecture is a very slow form of expression. It's like language. If you start talking in a totally impossible way so nobody understands what you are saying, they will react to you by saying "what's wrong with you?" But when they learn that language slowly, they can understand that you are

fig. 6
Fleinvaer Refugium
(Photo: Pasi Aalto)

saying really beautiful things. So, that's architecture.

D: One key word is meaningful. Which connects with what Sami is saying. It may sound weird in the beginning, but after a while it becomes meaningful. It makes sense, in a way. In the long run, if you manage to create a meaningful environment, it's good architecture—in my opinion.

L2: There's a trend I think—I've been in architecture school for a year and a half so I can't talk super broadly—towards the larger-scale project and wanting to make things regional. But it seems that a lot of your projects are very small-scale and that's intentional. Can you speak to why this is?

L1: Or if it is intentional.

L2: Or if it's intentional or if you feel like your ideals—or whatever it is—are at odds with the larger scale projects.

D: One explanation could be that we have been kind of outspoken about the capitalist forces in architecture defining the situation and conditions in society. We are just not getting these large-scale projects because people don't want to work with us. But, that's probably not a very good explanation, because we are getting larger, bigger clients gradually. I think that it connects more to the platform that we started with. We started with the design-build projects during our studies, and once we finished, we continued in that way. Sami in Finland and I in Norway.

So, we kept it going. Our creativity continued with really, really small budgets. Which was, in many ways, very closely connected with the art world. Projects started emerging from the boundary between art and architecture with relatively small budgets. We have kept our foot on this platform; we have never made any event of getting away from it because these are the most interesting projects that are in the world of architecture. Clients are good, and the environments we are working with are very interesting.

L2: Is there a point at which you feel like the project has a mind of its own?

D: Yeah, yeah. Definitely.

S: I remember hearing sometimes students say, "I want to do this, and I want to do that." That's a little bit worrisome, because at some point the project starts to tell you what it wants. And that's when you're on a good track.

D: And if you don't allow the project to take its own turns, you are maybe forcing it too much. So, I think that connects also to part of our work—that we have been overly interested in a contextual approach. Maybe it's an obsession we have. But, in many ways, it pays off in the design process because you are getting so much information and feedback from the weirdest things you discover in the research process … um, yeah, so, where were we?

L2: The question had a mind of its own.

D: So, it takes its own turns because of the context, which is always suggesting things. Yeah, that's what it was.

S: I think architecture is like research, or a journey to unknown places. Every project you do is an exploration …

—

Waitress: Y'all still doing okay over here?

[mumbling]

—

L1: Should we talk about animals?

L2: Yes.

L1: Okay, this is changing it up a little bit. We were curious about what you think about animals in relation to architecture. You've described [the UVA pavilion] in terms of animals—it's two fish crawling up the stairs, or a bug on a thing—and I know it's sometimes just a silly metaphor, but I was wondering if there was something real there. I'm thinking in terms of how a building relates

to a site or how a building can become a character or have a certain tone.

S: A nice thing about architecture is that it can be many things at the same time. So, one thing is it's an object. A big object, usually. It has interiority, that's also a nice thing to work with and think about—with all the views and the light and everything. But it's also, I think, very interesting to think about it as a sign in the landscape. And that sign always means something whether you want it to or not. And it's very nice to work with that sign—how it looks, what it does in the landscape, what kind of associations it brings. Human beings are observing the landscape and all the time trying to read it. *What is this? What does it do?* Not just what kind of object is it, but who is it? So, you give a kind of personality to a house, too. This is a very interesting thing. Some architects are very good at making architecture very strongly something—some kind of animal or personality. I think it's missing in many buildings today—that many architects don't give any kind of personality in the landscape for their building.

D: My professor from Oslo—Christian Norberg-Schulz—talked about how we project our bodily functions onto architecture. And Juhani Pallasmaa also talks about this—how your understanding of the world is about objects around you, how the façade and the skin of the building starts to represent the way you are feeling about things, how the openings of the buildings—the windows—become the eyes, and so on. There's nothing strange about it. It's very natural that we are projecting our feelings onto buildings. One can look at architecture and almost start to vomit, because it's giving a bad feeling. And, on the opposite side of the scale, it can give you a good feeling. So, talking about the skin, the fish scales—to us it's very natural, it's a fundamental thing about our built environment.

D: The skeleton, the structural system; the electricity, the nervous system; etcetera, etcetera.

—

Waitress: Would you like another one?

S: I feel but … I also think.

[laughter]

Waitress: Okay, I'll go put in another one.

—

L2: Should we do lightning round?

L1: Oh, maybe, "sum it up."

L2: Okay, describe your approach in one word.

fig. 9
Napkin sketch by the interviewees of
what they had for lunch

D: Okay, I would say—impossible.

[crowd oohs]

S: Perkele.

[Dagur and Sami laughing]

L2: Perkele? What? What is that?

D: Fucking shit.

[laughter]

L2: It's very mischievous.

S: It's actually a very old Finnish swear word, so it's difficult to translate. It's the most famous Finnish word.

L1: Okay, now lightning round. You have 30 seconds to answer each of these questions.

[pause]

L1: What's in your pockets?

D: Telephone and credit card.

S: Yeah, same.

L2: Nothing else? You have a lot of pockets.

[Sami pulls out pencils, measuring tape, an extremely large knife]

L2: What's the last thing you threw away?

D: The container of what I drew on the napkin.

S: A piece of oak.

L1: Favorite band in high school?

D: Joy Division.

S: Lynyrd Skynyrd.

L2: What's your zodiac sign?

D: Aquarius.

S: Virgin … Virgo.

L1: What did you want to be when you were growing up?

D: A pilot.

S: I'm still growing up, so I don't know.

L2: Okay, what would you be if you couldn't be an architect?

D: I'm guessing we have the same answer to that.

L1: Say it on "three": one, two, three …

D: Director. / S: A filmmaker.

L1: Favorite tree?

D: Gingko.

S: Juniper.

L2: Get ready for this question, 'cause it's weird. Largest animal you've ever killed?

D: A big fish.

S: I haven't killed any big animals. Maybe a seal.

L2: Weird question following that, but guilty pleasure?

[laughter]

S: Ah, let it come out. It's a long list. Guilty pleasure? There are only guilty pleasures in this world.

D: I have no guilty pleasures.

S: It's hard to feel guilty really about any pleasure.

L1: Okay this is the last question.

L2: Final question. Should I just ask? I'll ask. Which is better—cats or dogs?

D: Cats.

L2: Yes, we knew.

D: I have six cats.

S: I should have said dogs, but I have a cat now so I'm learning to understand cats, too.

D: And your cat is the size of my six cats.

S: Yes, it's the largest cat in the world—Maine Coon. But it's very dog-like.

L1: What's the cat's name?

S: Jonathan.

"The desire to live is a political decision. We do not want a world in which the guarantee that we will not die of starvation is bought by accepting the risk of dying of boredom."

– Raoul Vaneigem, *The Revolution of Everyday Life*

Epilogue

In his book *Trickster Makes This World*, literary scholar Lewis Hyde links the character of Trickster with the concept of appetite:

1

Lewis Hyde, *Trickster Makes This World: Mischief, Myth, and Art* (New York: Farrar, Strauss and Giroux, 1998), 17.

> *The trickster myth derives creative intelligence from appetite. It begins with a being whose main concern is getting fed and it ends with the same being grown mentally swift, adept at creating and unmasking deceit, proficient at hiding his tracks and at seeing through the devices used by others to hide theirs. Trickster starts out hungry, but before long he is master of the kind of creative deception that, according to a long tradition, is a prerequisite of art.*[1]

As the editors of a journal that calls itself *lunch*, we think about food quite a bit: food as the agent of both action and leisure, the impetus to get going as well as a reason to slow down, the locus of both toil and luxury—a decadent necessity, perpetually being churned into primary energy. Appetite, that mysterious property of vitality, runs through everything equally, a kind of democratic alternative to more inherently moralistic, perhaps less universally accessible motivations—like "hope," for example, or "duty."

Of course, the state of things *is* very serious: this we wholeheartedly acknowledge. Yet the ever-tightening finger trap of our noblest intentions requires above all a good goosing now and then, perhaps at no better time than the thirteenth hour when everything looks, at last, to be lost. At a time and place of the utmost gravity—in Charlottesville, Virginia, in 2018—we hope our thirteenth issue can serve as a reminder to stay loose, and funny, and hungry.

Contributors

ROSS EXO ADAMS is an assistant professor of Architecture and Urban Theory at the College of Design, Iowa State University. His research looks at the history and politics of urbanization, and he has published and presented widely on relations between architecture, urbanism, geography, political theory, ecology, and histories of power. He has exhibited work in, among others, the Venice Biennale and The Storefront for Art and Architecture. He has taught at the Bartlett School of Architecture at University College London, the Architectural Association, the Berlage Institute in Rotterdam, and the University of Brighton and has been a Fellow at the MacDowell Colony. Currently he is Reviews Editor for *The Journal of Architecture*. His monograph, *Circulation and Urbanization*, is forthcoming this year.

KRISTI CHERAMIE is an associate professor and the chair of undergraduate studies in landscape architecture at Ohio State University. Her research employs alternate practices of spatial history to explore erasure, loss, and forgetting as powerful agents of change in the landscape.

PHOEBE CRISMAN and MICHAEL PETRUS are urban flâneurs—by day (and night) teaching at the University of Virginia and practicing architecture and urbanism as Crisman+Petrus Architects. Inseparable since their studies at Carnegie Mellon and the Harvard Graduate School of Design, they like to write, draw, design, and build things together. They explore relationships between seemingly oppositional conditions: ecology and industry, regional watersheds and roofing details, climate change and craft. Collaborating with NGOs, businesses, and government agencies, they design strategies that foster thriving ecosystems, human cultures, and urban opportunity.

FREDI DEVAS is a wildlife filmmaker who cares deeply about the natural world and the challenges it faces. After completing a PhD on Chacma baboons in Namibia, Fredi did research on the bushmeat trade in Equatorial Guinea and then spent time living with the San bushmen in Southern Africa. Having worked on *Meerkat Manor* and *Nick Baker's Weird Creatures*, he joined the BBC to work on *Frozen Planet* and then *Wild Arabia*. On *Planet Earth II*, he decided to leave the wildernesses behind to produce and direct the "Cities" episode. Highlights included filming langurs and macaques in India and hyenas roaming the streets in Ethiopia, where he was struck by the harmonious relationship between people and the potentially dangerous animals with whom they share their cities.

JENNA DEZINSKI and JOHN PAUL RYSAVY are founding directors of the architecture and design collaborative And-Either-Or in Brooklyn, New York. Their practice is engaged in the research and design of buildings and objects with interest in the correlative between architecture and landscape, singular and plural, subject and object, culture and meaning. Their work has been published variously online and in print in *Pidgin*, *WLA*, and *Interior Design Magazine*, among others.

AUSTIN EDWARDS holds a Master of Architecture from the University of Virginia School of Architecture. Prior to his enrollment as a graduate student, he attended Auburn University, where he graduated *summa cum laude* with a B.S. in Aerospace Engineering. He has also previously worked at NASA Marshall Space Flight Center, where he was awarded for his design work.

DAGUR EGGERTSSON and SAMI RINTALA are the founders of Rintala Eggertsson Architects, a Norway based architecture firm, which bases its activities around furniture design, public art, architecture, and urban planning. In 2008 Eggertsson and Rintala were joined by Vibeke Jenssen who is now a full partner in the company. All three studied under Juhani Pallasmaa in Helsinki, and are informed by his phenomenological and cross-disciplinary thinking. Since the establishment in 2007, Rintala Eggertsson Architects have developed projects around the world and their work has been exhibited at the Maxxi Museum in Rome, Victoria & Albert Museum in London, the Venice Biennale, and the National Art Museum of China, amongst others. Eggertsson and Rintala have taught architecture in Europe, Australia and North-America and are currently Gensler Visiting Professors at Cornell University in New York.

BRADLEY L. GARRETT is a cultural geographer at the University of Sydney. An expert on cities, infrastructure, and social issues, he has published over 50 academic journal articles and book chapters. He also writes for several newspapers and magazines, including *Guardian Cities*, where he pens a sporadic column about public space. He is the author of *Explore Everything: Place-Hacking the City*, an account of his adventures trespassing into ruins, tunnels, and skyscrapers in eight different countries. He is currently at work on his fifth book entitled *Bunker: The Architecture of Dread*. The book follows communities preparing for the apocalypse.

KYLE J GENAME is a Master of Landscape Architecture candidate at the University of Virginia. His academic interests include gender and queer theory, fabric and textiles, plant biology, and horticulture.

MARGARETHA HAUGHWOUT's personal and collaborative artwork explores the intersections between ideas of technology and wilderness, digital networks and the urban commons, cybernetics and whole systems permaculture—in the context of ecological, technological and human survival. Her active collaborations include the Guerrilla Grafters: an art/activist group who graft fruit bearing branches onto non-fruit bearing, ornamental fruit trees, and the Coastal Reading Group: consisting of artists from different coasts who trouble the subjects of wilderness, speciation, humanness and ways of knowing through diverse engagements with nonhumans.

ANDREW HOLDER is a human being who teaches at Harvard University and has a practice in California. He is interested in how eighteenth-century German rococo prefigures new possibilities for contemporary architecture. This is almost, but not quite, all-absorbing enough to distract him from an abiding terror of not getting tenure and dying alone.

SAM JOHNSON is a Master of Architecture candidate at the University of Virginia. Prior to attending graduate school, he worked in New York City, where he also performed comedy. Aisha Sawatsky, Darcy Engle, Emily Fiedler, Katie LaRose & Sherry Ng are Master of Architecture candidates at the University of Virginia. Angela DeGeorge & Ann Le are Master of Architecture candidates at Parsons School of Design.

KATIE KELLY is a Master of Landscape Architecture candidate at the University of Virginia.

JOEL KERNER is a registered architect based in Chicago. He holds a Master of Architecture from SCI-Arc and a Bachelor of Arts from Judson University. He has contributed to broader design discourse through speculative projects, workshops, and serving as a lecturer and visiting critic. His work and writing has been exhibited in the U.S., France, Norway, and Estonia, and has appeared in *Onramp*, *Engawa*, *NAAM*, *PLAT*, and *POSIT*, among others.

ESTHER LESLIE is a professor of political aesthetics at Birkbeck, University of London. She currently likes to think about artificial colors, liquid crystals, fogs, froths, and foam, and most of what she does circles around the figure of Walter Benjamin, who, by the way, often felt himself dogged by the Bucklicht Männlein, or "Little Hunchback," whose signature was mischief and whom he never saw, but was only seen by. As may we all be.

KATE LIPKOWITZ is a Master of Architecture candidate at the University of Virginia and an alum of the University of Chicago.

NAOMI MAKI is an architectural designer based in New York City. She has practiced in Boston, Berlin, and New York. Her interest in the intersection of art and architecture led her to Sarah Oppenheimer's studio, where as lead project director, she is currently engaged in the design and fabrication of architectural sculptures and kinetic interventions of various scales and type. She received her Bachelor of Design in Architecture from the University of Florida and her Master of Architecture from the Harvard Graduate School of Design.

MARC MILLER is an assistant professor in the Department of Landscape Architecture at the Pennsylvania State University. His research interests include novel approaches to making landscapes including soil fabrication and television. He has degrees in landscape architecture, architecture, fine arts, and art history.

ANNA MORRISON is a Master of Architecture candidate at the University of Virginia.

EVAN PAVKA is a Toronto-based writer, editor, and educator. He holds an Master of Architecture in Architectural History and Theory from McGill University and currently teaches design studio as well as contemporary design history.

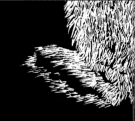

JULIAN RAXWORTHY, Ph.D., is a landscape architect from Australia. He is convenor of the Master of Landscape Architecture and Master of Urban Design programs at the University of Cape Town and in 2012 was a visiting professor at the University of Virginia.

RYAN ROARK, LAURA SALAZAR, and WEIWEI ZHANG are recent graduates of the Princeton School of Architecture's Master of Architecture program.

MATTHEW SEIBERT is a lecturer at City College of New York's Bernard and Anne Spitzer School of Architecture and co-founder of Landscape Metrics, a visualization studio built on an irreverence for disciplinary divisions.

ROSA CRISTINA CORRALES RODRIGUEZ, SHANNON RUHL, DONNA RYU, and MICHELLE STEIN, all having passed through University of Virginia's School of Architecture graduate program, came together through a mutual interest in proposing an altogether alternative architectural approach to the prompt of the U.S.-Mexico border wall. Currently operating from Honduras, Virginia, India, and New York, the design team hopes such a proposal expands the notion of our borders worldwide.

ARTÚR VAN BALEN examines the overlaps between visual arts, performance, and activism and founded the group Tools for Action in 2012. With Tools for Action he gives participatory skill-share workshops to art and activist groups as well as schools, teaching participants how to build inflatable sculptures and use them for political actions. On the side, he researches the development of inflatable art and technology, especially in the Soviet Union and the United States in the 1930s. He is currently co-curating the traveling exhibition *Floating Utopias* at the nGbK in Berlin.

DOMINIQUE VAN OLM is an emerging Canadian director and photographer. Her work documents the often complicated relationships people have with one another and themselves, exploring the human condition against the backdrop of the natural world. She has directed and photographed for companies such as The CBC, TIFF, Cosette, and BT/A. Her BFA thesis film, *Flower Girl*, has screened globally at festivals in Europe, South America, and Asia. She likes telling stories, riding her motorcycle, and seeing the world through her viewfinder.